# YOU CAN BE HEALED

*By Clara Palmer*

UNITY SCHOOL OF CHRISTIANITY
UNITY VILLAGE, MO.

This is one of a series of Unity books devoted to teaching how you can make your life better by applying Christian principles. The first Unity book, *Lessons in Truth,* was published in 1894 and is still in publication. The Unity work itself was established in 1889, when its founders, Charles and Myrtle Fillmore, began to share with others the Truth that had helped them.

The Unity movement now reaches millions of persons all over the world. Unity School of Christianity includes the Silent Unity department, to which thousands of people each year write for prayers for any need, and the Publishing Department, which distributes the Unity books and magazines that carry the Unity message around the world. Unity centers and churches are located in many large cities.

## DEDICATION

*This book is dedicated to
Jesus Christ.*

*In His name it is directed to all who need healing, to all who wish to have friends or loved ones restored, to all who serve the sick, to all who have been healed.*

## FOREWORD

Because I was healed through prayer although my condition had been termed hopeless, because I have personally witnessed the healing of incurable diseases and have read letters from hundreds who have been restored to health, I know that you can be healed.

Silent Unity prayed with me. Jesus Christ restored me. The workers in Silent Unity will pray with you without ceasing if you will write to them. They will answer your letter and instruct you in the way of Truth so that you may know the fullness of life, harmony, and light that are yours in Christ.

Much of this book was originally published as articles in *Weekly Unity*. Many readers reported receiving benefits from the healing blessings and requested their publication in book form. Their names, love, appreciation, and prayers, although invisible, are interwoven into every chapter. May God eternally bless them, and you too, with His healing life and wholeness.

*Clara Palmer*

# CONTENTS

| | |
|---|---|
| *Foreword* | 5 |
| The Temple Beautiful | 11 |
| Blessed Are Your Eyes | 14 |
| Blessed Are Your Ears | 19 |
| The Gateway of Life (Nose) | 25 |
| Year-Round Health (Colds) | 28 |
| Sanctuary of the Word (Mouth) | 30 |
| Spiritual Dentistry | 34 |
| Unsealed Lips (Speech) | 37 |
| The Power of the Voice | 39 |
| Two Valuable Sentinels (Tonsils) | 42 |
| The Wonder Shield (Thyroid Gland) | 44 |
| Mind Renewal | 46 |
| The Tree of Life (Spine) | 49 |
| God in Control (Epilepsy) | 52 |
| Relaxation | 55 |
| Life-Sustaining Breath (Lungs) | 59 |
| Bless Your Heart | 63 |
| Alive to Your Finger Tips (Capillaries) | 66 |
| Rhythmic Arterial Life | 69 |
| The Circuit of Life (Veins) | 72 |
| Blood of the Covenant | 76 |
| Commune with Your Lord | 80 |
| The Mediator (Blood Poisoning) | 82 |
| A Faithful Servant (Stomach) | 86 |
| Perfect Nutrition | 89 |
| Your Intelligent Liver | 93 |

| | |
|---|---|
| Perfect Elimination (Bowels) | 97 |
| Abiding Strength | 101 |
| The Great Repair Shop (Spleen) | 104 |
| Truth Sweetens and Restores (Pancreas) | 108 |
| Restoration of Kidneys | 112 |
| Divinely Directed (Bladder) | 115 |
| Body Renewal (Bones) | 119 |
| Joyous and Free (Joints) | 122 |
| Responsibility (Shoulders) | 125 |
| Encircling Love (Arms) | 128 |
| Your Helpful Hands | 130 |
| Independence (Hips) | 133 |
| Devotion and Humility (Knees) | 136 |
| Two Blessed Feet | 138 |
| Strong Wrists and Ankles | 142 |
| Perfect Co-ordination (Muscles) | 145 |
| Healing Blessing (Nerves) | 148 |
| The Solar Plexus (Emotions) | 151 |
| The Silence | 154 |
| The Generative Organs | 158 |
| Busy Manufacturers (Glands) | 164 |
| Healing Light (Cancer) | 167 |
| He Bindeth Up Wounds | 170 |
| The Seamless Robe (Skin) | 173 |
| Your Crown of Beauty (Hair) | 178 |
| Away with Epidemics! | 181 |
| Wholeness for You | 184 |

# YOU CAN BE HEALED

# *The Temple Beautiful*

YOUR BODY is a temple beautiful. It is the living temple of God. Every cell in your body should be radiant with light, love, and peace. When it is, you enjoy the perfect health that is God's will for you. The very joy of living animates you. You radiate the spirit of wholeness to others.

When any part of your body is out of harmony, uncomfortable, or diseased you can bless it with a living word of Truth and it will respond.

Frequently the question is asked "Should I hold a thought for entire wholeness or should I direct my attention to the seat of pain or disease?" There can be but one answer. You should direct your attention Godward, ever seeking to know and maintain your perfect unity with Him.

However if your experience happens to be the same as mine has been, you will find it helpful to take the word of affirmation or prayer that God will supply you with—either through direct inspiration in your own mind and heart or through the written or spoken word of others—and speak it in direct blessing to the part of your body that appears to be in the shadow of pain, disease, or weakness.

I like to think of faith as a flaming torch, and to use it, if need be, just as I might use a flashlight to locate the switch that will turn on the efficient and penetrating gleam of a more powerful light.

My faith directs me to Jesus Christ for healing. As soon as I contact Him in spirit my mind is filled with light, even as the darkened room is flooded with light when I press the button that my flashlight reveals.

I do not condemn a room for being dark. I praise God for the convenience of electricity whereby I may instantly produce light. Neither do I condemn any portion of my body or of any other person's body when it needs healing. I take my touch of faith that lights my way to Jesus Christ. By His loving help and power I turn on the healing light of Spirit. If need be I go with the light of His grace to every function in the body and speak the word of love and blessing.

There are many who respond at once to a thought of complete and perfect wholeness. There are others whose body cells are not so quick to respond. They seem to need specific, patient, and loving blessing. Doubt and fear or disbelief may extinguish the light so that it is necessary to turn it on more than once.

Such an occurrence need be no cause for discouragement. Rather it is a call to more valiant endeavor. When faithful, persistent effort is required and maintained it is a means of growth toward the stature of the perfect Christ. Through faithfulness

*The Temple Beautiful*

the character is molded. It becomes stabilized in Truth. The results may not be spectacular, but they are lasting and comforting. They build one up in confidence. They restore the mind as well as the body. They establish one in the consciousness of abiding health and eternal life.

Before you take up a healing blessing, it is well when possible to be quiet. Subject your thoughts to the love, faith, and peace of Jesus Christ. His faith, which is ever active in you, effaces all anxiety. His love dissolves all fear or inharmony. His peace allays pain, relaxes every nerve, tendon, and muscle. Thus His healing life is permitted to flow freely through you. His life is the light of man. "Let there be light."

# Blessed Are Your Eyes

THE EYE is a physical refractor of light, the organ of vision that makes one conscious of the outer light, and enables one to see the things of the outer world. Directly connected with the brain by the optic nerve, the eye in its ability to see is dependent on the brain. By its quick telegraphic response, it is the brain that rights the objects that are focused upside down on the retina. The actual seat of visual sensation is in the brain. Thus we learn how promptly our God-inspired intelligence can instantly right even the most topsy-turvy appearances.

The eye speaks all languages. Eyes give life to the thoughts we think, the words we speak, the emotions we feel. They are the windows of the mind. Outer things are revealed to the mind by them, and the thoughts of the mind are reflected in them. Thoughts animated and illumined by the light of love, joy, faith, or noble purpose brighten the eyes with friendliness, cheer, and good will. On the other hand, cruel, greedy, bold, or brazen thoughts harden them. Thoughts of fear, desolation, and hopelessness make them lusterless, while thoughts of dishonesty and suspicion make them shifty and inquiet. Thus we may discern how intimately the

## Blessed Are Your Eyes 15

eyes are related to the word or the thought and how readily they will respond to thoughts or words of faith, vision, light, and perfection.

When sight is reinforced by spiritual vision the eyes regain or maintain their perfection. Eyes of those who constantly turn to God are always beautiful and full of light. As Tennyson wrote, "eyes are homes of silent prayer."

The eye is so constructed that it relaxes more when looking into the distance than when doing close work, such as sewing, reading, and the like. For this reason it is beneficial to raise the eyes occasionally from close work and let them rest comfortably on something in the distance.

The Psalmist decided wisely when he said, "I will lift up mine eyes unto the hills." If you find that your eyes are tiring, close them for just a moment. When one wishes to enter the silence, the closing of the eyes symbolizes the closing of the "inner door" of spirit against the intrusion of outer affairs.

Eyelids are protective in more ways than one. Close your eyes a moment. Let your mind relax. Cast your burdens on the Lord. Now think a thought such as this: *I will lift up my eyes unto God, from whom comes my perfect sight.* Then open your eyes and let them rest on space. Soon you will learn to look beyond the limitations of the personal man, his fears and his problems. Your consciousness will reach upward into the infinitude of the Christ Mind and you will see, know, and follow the way of divine light and vision.

Cross-eye can be straightened by relaxing both eyes and mind and letting them rest in the harmonizing, adjusting peace of God. Declare: *My eyes are straightened and my path is made clear before me as I rest in the peace of God.* If you have a child whose eyes are crossed, speak this word of blessing for him as you tuck him into bed at night.

When rays of light are not refracted perfectly by the eye we find conditions known as farsightedness, nearsightedness, or astigmatism. If you are troubled with any of these conditions, turn trustingly to God. Ask Him to make you perfectly receptive to His light and inspiration. Do not condemn glasses or those who wear them. Neither resist wearing them nor permit yourself to feel that you are dependent on them. Avoid discussing poor eyesight. Seek in every way to be receptive to God's light. He can and will free you from glasses, and perfect your eyes as rapidly as you are able and willing to accept and use the light of Truth.

Bless your eyes and your mind, saying, *Teach me Thy way, dear God. Let my eyes, my mind, my heart be receptive to Thy light. Let Thy light shine through them perfectly.*

Race thoughts that decree that age is likely to be accompanied by failing vision, that eyeballs harden, that spots form covering or destroying the

### Blessed Are Your Eyes 17

sight, that eyelids droop or become red-rimmed, that tear ducts close misting the vision, will everyone give way before the clear, ringing declaration of Jesus Christ, who with divine authority proclaimed, "Blessed are your eyes, for they see."

Accept these precious words of Jesus from the indwelling sanctuary of your soul where He abides. He is blessing you with light, perfecting your vision. Acknowledge His light. Let it shine in your mind and radiate through your thoughts and words. Answer Jesus in faith, believing: *Blessed are my eyes for they see.*

When through your acceptance of His faith and love you permit His light to shed its glory in your mind and heart, things appear differently to you. Love shines through old fear or bitterness and their dark shadow is dissolved. Faith shines through doubt and disbelief and all sense of darkness, confusion, and imperfect vision is lifted.

The eye of God that looks out through you always sees good. Your physical eye responds to His perfect vision, and behold! "blessed are your eyes, for they see."

No thought of cataracts or eyespots can curtain your eyes, no thought of age can weaken, dim, or blur them, no thought of physical infection or inheritance can make or keep them imperfect when you consecrate your eyes to God and let His vision be your vision.

Looking on the world through God-perfected eyes you find your world transformed. God pronounces a benediction of love, harmony, and beauty through you upon all that you see.

"The precepts of Jehovah are right, rejoicing the heart:

The commandment of Jehovah is pure, enlightening the eyes."

Work with God. Let the fullness of His life, love, and Truth become established in your consciousness and you will master every fear thought of age, darkness, or doubt.

Your eyes look forth through the prism of God's pure love and light. They are blessed with perfection. Look now and see the beauty and goodness of God. Behold His omnipresence.

*"Blessed are your eyes, for they see."*

# Blessed Are Your Ears

How accurately the master violinist tunes his instrument! He has trained his sense of hearing in perfect accord with the tones he would reproduce. How blessed are his ears!

Your life is the blessed instrument God has intrusted to you. You can so train your ears to listen to His harmony within you and about you that you will reproduce its melody and rhythm and beauty in all your ways. "Blessed are . . . your ears, for they hear."

While the eyes report the light rays to the brain for interpretation, the ears function quite as effectively in sending the sound waves to the brain over the auditory nerve. They help to co-ordinate the sounds of the outer world with the divine symphony of the inner life.

There is a perfect auditory chamber in the ear. Highly sensitive to all sound waves, it has much to do with the sense of rhythm and equilibrium. Therefore it is always well to bless the ear with thoughts of the perfect poise and balance of mind that is ours in Christ.

Five openings are found in the middle ear. One leads to the Eustachian tube opening into the pharynx, linking the ear with the throat. It reminds us of the words of Paul, "Faith *cometh* by hearing, and hearing by the word of God." Two openings lead to the inner ear, one to the outer, and one to the mastoid antrum. It is interesting to note that the word mastoid was derived from Greek words meaning "shaped like a breast."

It has been written that the eyes and the ears represent the parental faculties of the mind. The eyes perceive the light. The ears through the play of sound waves conceive the word and make its formation possible in the consciousness of man.

There were a number of Bible characters who we are told walked and talked with God. Today we have teachers of Truth who are in such constant communion with the Father that outer noise never disturbs or confuses them. Through concentration and attentiveness to God's counsel they have been quickened in consciousness and they have been enabled to place a guard before the outer ear protecting it from all inharmony, enabling them to free their own lives and the lives of others from unrest and discord.

A student who was very sensitive to noise asked why God did not supply us with earlids, as well as eyelids, so that we might close our ears and shut out noise as readily as we close our eyes and shut out an obnoxious view. To such a one the counsel is, hold fast to peace. Let the unquiet be as unquiet as they will. Turn to the retreat of the silence within

## Blessed Are Your Ears

you. There you will find the creative word clothed in the stillness of His peace.

Cultivate listening inwardly as well as outwardly and the counsel of God will gently come to you. Every word, every sound from without will receive the blessing of His peace and nothing will disturb you. Remember there are two openings leading to the inner ear, whereas there is but one leading to the outer ear.

Trying to deaden one's thoughts in excessive noise is as unwise and intemperate as trying to drown them in alcohol. In many instances it is even more unkind. Especially in cases of babies and small children, how thoughtlessly adults say, "Oh, they don't mind"! Then later they return to us asking, "Why are my children so inattentive and heedless?" They have been forced by circumstances to pay no attention to noise from loud radios, banging doors, raucous voices, hooting horns. Ears have been overworked during study periods and during sleeping as well as waking hours by the need of shutting out noise. Every child, every adult should have a period of quiet when the mind is trained to listen to the inner promptings of Spirit. The child or adult who is attentive to God is able to concentrate, to hear the things he should hear, to reason things out. He is naturally obedient and successful.

In cases of earache or of mastoiditis just know within yourself that the ear that needs soothing, purifying, healing is pressed tenderly against the bosom of infinite love. Keep this thought uppermost in your mind until relief is received. It won't take long if your faith is centered in the healing power of Jesus Christ. *Divine love is healing you now. In the peace and quietness of God's presence your ear, your mind, are cleansed and freed from all sense of disease, pain, or confusion. Divine peace blesses you. Divine love heals you now.*

Your ears are blessed, harmonious, functioning perfectly. No sound can disturb you. You are poised and centered in the peace of God.

Whether you desire your mind to be opened so that you may know God's voice and recognize His word, or whether you seek the healing of the outer ear so that you may hear the voices of those about you, the healing Christ gives you this assurance: "Blessed are . . . your ears, for they hear."

Listen for the loveliness that is coming into your life upon waves of sound. Listen for the finer things that quicken the noble impulses within you. Listen for God's harmony of love. Drink it into your soul. Pour it forth into your life.

Over the infinite ocean of God life and substance waves of faith, joy, and harmony are bearing your good to you. Within your ear is a perfect receiving chamber forever resounding the message the waves bring to you. One part of your inner ear is even shaped like a tiny, reverberating shell.

*Blessed Are Your Ears* 23

To what do you listen? Stop and think. Do you listen to the voice of love? Do you listen to the assurance of substance and success? Do you heed God's counsel of order, wisdom, faith, and loving-kindness? Do you hear the trill of joy sounding through nature's domain? Listen to the whispered prayer of the breeze in the tree branches. Do you not catch the assurance that God is in His world and all is well? Of course you do! "Blessed are . . . your ears, for they hear." Your ears are opened, harmonized, and healed this moment by the power of Jesus Christ.

Blessed are your ears! They are an open portal through which your mind receives. When you listen to good reports, wholesome words, clean, happy, constructive things, you are listening to God.

Consecrate your ears to God. Listen for His indwelling voice. It will come to you from the stillness of your own heart, you will hear its cadences of love, joy, faith, and life sounding through the voices of those who love you and who love God. It will reveal to you the good that is working through the minds, hearts, and lives of all people.

Jesus met the condemnation that the scribes and Pharisees voiced against the woman taken in adultery by stooping quietly and writing in the sand. As He wrote He listened to the inner voice of divine love, and when He arose He spoke but fourteen words, and the accusing crowd slunk away. His ears were closed to evil reports.

Should someone come to you eager to voice trivial, unclean, untrue, or unkind things, quietly, lovingly let him know that you have consecrated your ears to God and do not choose to listen to such talk, because you want your hearing to remain unobstructed and perfect. Your ears will be quickened and blessed. Your friend will be prevented from saying things that he might regret.

Your ears are healed that they may hear wise counsel, good reports, happy messages of Truth that will bless your mind, life, and environment with the peace, love, harmony, and joy of God.

"Blessed are . . . your ears, for they hear."

# The Gateway of Life

BY ITS nasal cavities, ducts, and olfactory nerve, the nose is closely connected with the eyes, the organ of vision; the ears, the organ of hearing; the mouth, the organ of taste; the brain, the seat of intelligence; the voice, the instrument of the word, and the lungs, the vital center of respiration.

I like to think of the nose as the gateway of life, the two nostrils revealing to me the close parallel course of the natural and the spiritual life. God "breathed into his nostrils the breath of life; and man became a living soul." The holy breath of God functioning in you redeems you from sin, sickness, and death. It establishes you in newness of life and perfection of being.

Let us again consider the close connection between the nose and the eyes, ears, brain, mouth, throat, and lungs. Notice how directly the inspiration, the life of Spirit, is sent to the vital centers of intelligence, respiration, and speech with every breath you draw.

How do you think of your nose? Have you appreciated it as a vital channel of life? When you do you will breathe in the very breath of the Almighty. You will know that the living substance of God permeates the atmosphere surrounding you and you will discern how with every breath you draw the pure substance of Spirit is built into your body.

Instinct, intuition, discernment are linked in thought with the functions of the nose. These are protective and good in their places, but when misused they become a nuisance, as in the case of the "nosy" person or of the one who is forever getting a "hunch" that things are all wrong. There are many lessons the nose may teach.

If you would test the close connection of the function of inspiration with your thinking faculty, go to a window. Especially when you have been sitting at work in a close room trying to think, throw up the window sash and breathe in several breaths of fresh air. Note the immediate enlivening of your brain. Oxygen is required by every living creature.

Now give thanks for the sense of smell. Food flavors are enhanced by it, the enjoyment of gardens doubled, the subtle essence of spring apprehended. The nose supplements the sense of taste and adds much to the joy of living.

Through the nostrils we learn something of the sweet savor of life as it ascends from garden, forest, earth, and sea. Likewise the very essence of Spirit arises from within you, from your true self. Paul said, "We are a sweet savor of Christ unto God."

It has been written of certain of the saints that a

## The Gateway of Life

fragrance as of daintiest flowers emanated from them. Certain characteristics do emanate from the body, some in shadows, some in light, some in subtle odors. Watch the dog when a stranger approaches. Even before the animal can see him, it will sniff the air and growl in disapproval or wag its tail in friendliness. Many diseases may be diagnosed by their odor; then why not clean, wholesome life?

Let the very essence of the Christ life flow through you in courage, love, and understanding.

As the sweetness of your Lord thus goes out from you, the loveliness of all nature will respond to you. No flower that God ever created can cause hay fever to attack you when you realize that the chalice of every blossom is pouring forth the essence of life. God breathes the breath of life through all His creation.

Bless your nose, saying: *The breath of the Almighty has given me life. My nostrils, nasal cavities, and sinuses are clear and clean. I breathe freely. My thoughts are inspired and my mind renewed. I discern the purity, the living substance, and lovingkindness of Jesus Christ now manifesting themselves in me. I am blessed by His grace. The incense of His Holy Spirit ascends within me. I am radiant with life.*

# *Year-Round Health*

GOD IN THE midst of you is life! His life flows freely through you. It permeates the air you breathe, the food you eat, and is constantly renewing every cell in your body.

Colds have no part nor place in your life.

No part of your body is more wonderfully constructed or carefully protected than the respiratory tract. You need not fear winter air. As it passes through your nose it is filtered, moistened, warmed, made ready for your lungs. Just one brisk walk in bracing winter weather will prove to you how vitalizing it is. No air-conditioning invention of man can compare with the nasal passages.

Bless your nose with an appreciative thought. Thank God for the divinely intelligent way in which your respiratory organs are protected.

Every breath you draw betokens your eternal alliance with life. Enjoy the winter months. Breathe freely, walk joyously, live fearlessly. Build up a year-round consciousness of health.

Colds reveal a general systemic denial of life. All too frequently they are nonchalantly accepted as something uncomfortable but of small importance, a winter inconvenience that is inevitable and must be endured. Thus does man let go of the divine life principle that would sustain him in perfect health.

Vital, pure, upbuilding, the substance of life is yours to appropriate, understand, and enjoy. Charles Fillmore teaches that the nose represents the initiative capacity of the mind. Be willing to launch out, to declare your disbelief in colds, to free yourself and thereby help to free the race from depleting "cold" habits.

Dress suitably, eat sensibly, think wisely. Talk health in order that your mode of living may bear out your faith in God as your health. Rely fearlessly on the life, substance, and intelligence of your God-inspired being.

Meet any sense of fear, negation, drafts, chilliness, or lassitude with a strong, positive avowal of life. Hold no thought of condemnation toward yourself, others, circumstances, or the weather. Deny the appearance of any physical symptoms of a cold and assert your nonbelief in them, but do not waste energy fighting them.

Relax. Rest quietly and confidently in the consciousness that God is all-pervading life as you affirm: *Life of God, I welcome you. Every nerve, muscle, bone, and cell in my body welcomes you. I yield myself completely to the restorative power of the Holy Spirit. I am fearless, happy, strong, and free.*

# *Sanctuary of the Word*

IN THE heart of a great city stands on old church. Its once tall spire appears like a bit of sharpened kindling against the background of skyscrapers. From within the church the steadily burning altar light sends its beckoning gleam out through ancient windows. One may enter there at any time, quietly nestle down in a pew and feed both mind and soul with spiritual thoughts, or drop on one's knees before the altar rail and seek God's help and will concerning one's immediate affairs.

Closely joined to your heart in spiritual functioning, there is a sanctuary that reminds me of the church in the midst of the city thoroughfare. As you grow in understanding and appreciation of its power, as you utilize its possibilities, it will save you and help you to save others from much physical and mental stress, pain, remorse, and sorrow.

It is as Solomon said,

"Whoso keepeth his mouth and his tongue
Keepeth his soul from troubles."

Just as one can feel the power of God in the atmosphere of the church and gain spiritual mastery and peace by pausing there to seek God's counsel, so one may feel the power of the word which is centralized physically in the mouth. Charles Fillmore

## Sanctuary of the Word

teaches that the seat of power is at the root of the tongue.

Within the mouth the teeth stand ever ready with the help of tongue and facial muscles to break up the food and prepare it for the stomach. A wise person never swallows his food whole. Neither does he release the first hasty thought that comes into his mind, nor let the opinions of others affect him on the spur of the moment. He analyzes his words before he lets them go, avoiding inharmony that might prove even more troublesome than a toothache. He weighs the opinions of others before he judges them.

The tongue is the servant of the physical man, the organ of taste that so finely discriminates between various foods. Perhaps the opportunity to know and to practice God's will, to gain perfect control of yourself, is not quite so great in any part of the body as it is in the function of taste. Taste applies not alone to the food you like but also to the company you choose, the surroundings you prefer, the clothes you wear, and the habits you form.

So we find that the tongue is closely related to the inner or soul consciousness and is both physical and spiritual in its functioning even as is the word of God.

Truth elevates the soul, illumines the mind, quickens discrimination. As a person grows Godward his taste changes. Grosser animal foods, stimulating drinks, narcotic drugs, tobacco, or passionate sense living in any form, which may appeal to the physical nature either by way of exciting or deadening the senses, he drops easily, painlessly, and completely.

Through redemption and control of our tastes we learn to fulfill God's perfect will of beauty, order, and harmony in our thoughts, desires, body, and environment.

Distinctive, spiritualized taste calls the perfection of the Christ into outer being. It is revealed in original thoughts and words of a high order. It gives character, grace, and loveliness to everything a person thinks, says, or does. It adds tone to life's expression. Here we find voice and tongue unified in a single purpose.

The tongue as the servant of the word is likewise the servant of God. There within your own mouth you find one way in which you are physically, mentally, spiritually, and eternally linked with Him.

Logically you want your life to yield the best fruit possible. You want to be surrounded by a lovely environment. You want to taste the sweetness of the blessings of your Lord. You want to know how to clothe your mind and body harmoniously and perfectly. You want to be free from every habit, shortcoming, desire, or disease that might hamper you or hold you down. You want to be even as God would have you be.

Be still and know your oneness with the perfect will of the Father.

Consider the infinite grace, the matchless taste of Jesus Christ.

Ponder upon the living Word, given expression through you, made flesh in you.

Use this affirmation: *My taste is made perfect in Christ. My desires are purified, my words are controlled by His Holy Spirit. I consecrate my mouth to Him. I eat, think, speak, and live in harmony with the divine law of order, love, purity, and wholeness.*

"A gentle tongue is a tree of life."

"Whoso keepeth his mouth and his tongue
Keepeth his soul from troubles."

# *Spiritual Dentistry*

BEFORE YOU go to your dentist, go to God. Your faith can be so quickened that you will prove the healing, restorative power of the Holy Spirit within you. Should you still feel that your teeth must have the attention of a dentist go to God first and become poised in Truth. Fortify yourself with the consciousness of God's ever-presence. Thus fear and dread will be minimized as you approach the dentist's chair. By keeping your thought poised and centered in the peace and harmony of God you can overcome the pain and discomfort sometimes experienced there.

In Truth God is the only perfect dentist, the only one who knows how to restore your teeth, how to heal pyorrhea, how to tighten your teeth, cleanse your gums, purify, and perfect your mouth.

There is no time or circumstance when God will not help you, whether it be to renew or restore your teeth, or to enable you to adjust yourself to plates or bridgework.

The teeth masticate the food and prepare it for digestion. They represent the analytical, discerning power of mind that lays hold of a thought and prepares it for assimilation and appropriation. Truth does not deprive a person of common sense. It quick-

## Spiritual Dentistry

ens him in cleanliness, order, and good judgment.

Teeth are covered by the hardest substance in the body. Nevertheless there is perhaps no other part of the body that reveals such tenacity in holding onto evidences of sickness, carelessness, neglect. About the first thing necessary in the healing of the teeth is to go behind every hard-shelled thought and cleanse the mind from the memory of previous illnesses, grudges, hard times, or lack.

When you brush your teeth, do you watch for and fear, soft, spongy, bleeding gums? Stop it. Ply your toothbrush to uplifting affirmations of life, purity, strength, and substance. Instead of watching for abnormal looseness or cavities, watch for the gleaming radiance of perfect enamel. Watch for firm gums, a clean mouth, beautiful teeth. Thank God for them. Appreciate your perfect teeth. Hold steadfastly to the knowledge that God is your abundant life. Conform your mode of living to your thoughts of Truth, and one of these days your smile will reveal the perfect teeth you have desired.

As you brush your teeth think dental health thoughts: *I joyously co-operate with the divine law of purity, cleanliness, and order. I give thanks for the perfect manifestation of God substance in my mind, body, and affairs. I rejoice in the sustaining thoughts of Truth constantly coming to me. I praise God for a clean mind, a pure heart, and a clean mouth blessed by strong, perfect, beautiful teeth.*

Be loyal to your divine inheritance of life and substance. For the prevention or filling of cavities affirm: *The ever-renewing life and substance of God is constantly rebuilding my teeth.*

Bless your gums with this thought: *I firmly believe in the pure, restorative life of God active in my gums. I give thanks that they are sound and whole.*

Cure the aching tooth by your faith-filled blessings: *God's will of health and peace is now established in me.*

If you are trying to adjust yourself to plates or bridgework think of them as the wonderful blessing that they are. Do not think of them as foreign to you, something false that does not belong to you. Accept them, wear them, use them. Unify yourself with them and know: *God in the midst of me is mighty to adjust my teeth in divine order and comfort. I give thanks that His perfect law is now fulfilled in me.*

Infold a teething baby in loving patience as you speak this word: *You are God's child of light and peace. Your life unfolds in orderly development. Your teeth are blessings of growth. They come forth easily in perfect formation. You are strong, healthy, happy, and content.*

# *Unsealed Lips*

JESUS unsealed the lips of the dumb and they spoke.

Christ in you gives you perfect and free expression. Through Him you can overcome any impediment or hesitancy in your speech, any inability to speak. "The word [of God] is very nigh unto thee, in thy mouth, and in thy heart, that thou mayest do it."

The word of God is the living expression of Christ in the midst of you. No retarding thought, no inhibiting fear, no sensitive, shut-in feeling of soul, no nervous, stammering haste can withstand the power of His spoken word of faith.

The word that Christ speaks through you is the living word of God. Blessed by the power of His Spirit, it opens the door of your inmost being, wells up in your heart and mind, fills your consciousness with its power, and unlocks your lips.

Your divinely appointed purpose is to express God. Fearlessly, gladly accept and know the freedom of Truth. It has unsealed your lips, freed your tongue from bondage, blessed your voice with the harmony of Spirit, touched your heart with the love of the Christ.

You are unbound, free, triumphant!

*I am unbound, free, triumphant!*

Think these words over again and again. Get the feeling of them. Shape them with your lips. Do not hurry. Take your time. Remember Christ is working through you.

*I am unbound, free, triumphant!*

As you let the words take form, relax. They will loosen your throat muscles and free your voice.

*I am unbound, free, triumphant!*

Try it again and yet again until you consciously feel the freeing power of God's grace blessing and opening your lips. He is with you now.

You have a message to give and you can give it. You have a word to speak and you can speak it. You have music peculiar to your own soul to express and you can express it.

Listen to the inner voice of Jesus Christ. It is the voice of your own spirit. Hear its soft cadences, note its tone of authority, feel its blessing of love, courage, and power, listen to its lilting joy.

Speak now, beloved, speak! Let the message of your heart go forth in the perfectly spoken word. "The word [of God] is very nigh unto thee, in thy mouth, and in thy heart, that thou mayest do it."

You are unbound, free, and triumphant!

# The Power of the Voice

THAT JESUS recognized the power of the voice is proved by His statement "My sheep hear my voice . . . and they follow me." He knew the volume of life and love that His voice gave forth.

That which was true of the voice of the Good Shepherd is true of your voice. Just as His words carried the sound of love, faith, authority, and assurance that drew the multitudes to Him and freed them from sin, sickness, hunger, and loneliness, so your words convey to others the feeling of your innermost self.

Watch your voice. You can make of it what you will. It has a far greater effect on your nervous system as well as on the nerves of others than you may realize.

The closer you live to Jesus Christ in thought and feeling the more your voice will take on the depth and quality of divine love and understanding. Even as the voices of children frequently grow in tone to be like the voices of those with whom they are closely associated, so your voice takes on the tone of your inner self.

It has been observed by a certain student of Truth that words of love, faith, and harmony spoken from the heart enrich the voice, tone up the vocal cords, soothe and heal laryngitis, cleanse and restore tonsils that are swollen or diseased.

What has been proved by another may be proved by you. It is easy to believe that a voice raised in angry, rasping arrogance or dispute irritates the throat, nasal, and aural passages.

A boy of seven was healed of mastoiditis by his grandmother. When asked what she did, she replied, "I prayed through the night as I worked over Bobby. He had not been able to hear for several days and the doctor feared that he might never hear again. He was in a very critical condition. I asked that the voice of the Good Shepherd might speak through me and that Bobby might hear the voice and answer it by getting well."

Notice now what the child said when he was asked about his healing. "Grandma's voice was like the sound of running water. First it stopped the burning in my head, then it made my earache better. Then I heard her call my name and I answered her." What a blessed memory that child will carry of the power of the voice of healing love!

Would you have a beautiful voice, one that stands for sincerity, helpfulness, peace, and Truth? Spend some time each day thinking about the tone of the inner Christ voice that speaks within your heart and inspires you with faith, hope, love, courage, and power to overcome. You can build into your voice so great a measure of divine peace and harmony that it will become as healing music to whoever hears it. It will prove an ever-present blessing to you, an eternal blessing to others.

In the meantime you will find that you have let go of ill temper, hasty, scolding words, rasping tones, uncertain nerves, swollen tonsils, and annoying sinus or nasal disturbances.

*I hear and follow the voice of Jesus Christ within my soul. It speaks through me in tones of love, peace, good will, divine power, and cheer. I consecrate my voice to Truth and use it for the uplift of man and to the glory of God. It is strong, harmonious, musical, and full of blessing. Praise God!*

# Two Valuable Sentinels

TWO SENTINELS are placed in the throat, one on either side. They register any invading infection and call out to you to purify your thoughts and establish yourself in wholesome, healthy habits.

Get acquainted with these two alert sentinels, your perfect tonsils. Make friends with them, and you will know them as protective agencies, physical safeguards against possible infection of ears, larynx, or lungs. Does it seem in order to have them removed when they are rendering faithful service in revealing a possible systemic condition that may need adjusting?

Tonsils have a definite and valuable service else they would not have been placed in the throat by an all-wise Creator. You would not break a barometer because it indicated an approaching storm.

When tonsils are swollen or inflamed you can avoid any further physical inharmony by surrendering yourself to the freeing, cleansing, healing power of the Christ, whose Holy Spirit is in you.

Tonsils are sensitive and very responsive. They react at once to cleansing, purifying thoughts and are restored to wholeness and perfection just as soon as the Holy Spirit is given a chance to do its perfect work in mind and body.

A good prayer to use is the word that Jesus spoke to the man who appealed to Him, saying, "Lord, if thou wilt, thou canst make me clean." Jesus answered, "I will; be thou made clean."

Jesus Christ is not two thousand years removed from you. He is with you now. His presence infolds you, His Spirit abides in you.

Go with Him now to every part of your body. Let His light shine clearly in your mind and heart. Speak to every function, organ, and cell, saying, "I will; be thou made clean." By this divine willing every organ and function of your body is cleansed and made whole.

Are you associated with some child whose tonsils need healing? Let the consciousness of the Great Physician fill your word with divine faith, love, and power as you bless the mind, heart, and tonsils of the child, saying, "I will; be thou made clean."

There is living power in the words of Jesus. The healing blessing given here will restore every part of your body temple, cleanse your thoughts, and make you as refreshed in mind and in body as is a garden after a much-needed rain.

By the power and authority of the Lord Jesus Christ His healing word is now given to all who are willing to receive: *"I will; be thou made clean."*

# The Wonder Shield

THE MORE faithfully you bless your body the more you will come to love it and to appreciate the wonder of its creation. There is a gland lying just below the pharynx that might be called the wonder shield of the body. Its function is to purify, to protect against unbalanced growth, to counteract the effects of excessive emotionalism. Its name is taken from the Greek word meaning "shield-shaped."

Since its function is becoming more generally known and recognized, man is beginning to realize the important work of this physical and mental balancer of the body. Physicians as well as metaphysicians are endeavoring to encourage people to work in harmony with the thyroid gland by controlling the emotions and the appetite.

Truth is a shield to all who use it. Nothing will more quickly help a person to control his disposition, appetite, desires, or emotions than Truth.

One person in a home, community, or nation who has gained perfect self-control helps all whom he contacts toward self-mastery. His perfect poise and balance increases their sense of peace and well-being. Nothing more greatly helps one who is suffering from thyroid disturbance, whether in the form

## The Wonder Shield

of a goiter, nervousness, excessive craving for food, undue emotionalism, unbalanced growth or otherwise, than a sense of peace and well-being. It was this that Jesus gave to the world.

Let all who desire help for goiter or thyroid trouble draw close to Jesus Christ. His healing gift has never been withdrawn. Let them be still before Him and learn of Him the lesson of mastery of self, the purification of mind, soul, and body by the indwelling Spirit. Let them receive from Him the gift of healing peace and power, the courage and fearlessness of divine faith and conviction.

Instead of fearing goiter let the verse from the Psalms "My shield is with God" become a healing prayer, a healing motive. Think of the thyroid gland as a physical shield provided by an all-wise Creator, for such it is. Bless it by establishing yourself in the mastery of Truth that makes you master of yourself. There is nothing for you to fear. "One is your master, *even* the Christ."

Be still and know: *"My shield is with God."* God can and is restoring you and every function in your body to perfect order, harmony, and health. Rise up in the authority of your Christ self and accept the shield of divine mastery, purity, peace, and wholeness.

*Be thou made whole.*

# Mind Renewal

THE HEAD may be likened to a tower of light from which the illumination of Divine Mind shines in blessing to every part of the body. Just as the light from a lighthouse will guide the captain of a ship to steer his craft away from the rocks, so the light of Truth shining through your mind will guide you away from error.

The brain is the seat of thinking, the organ through which the mind formulates its thoughts. Thinking is to the brain what exercise is to the muscles. Constructive, well-ordered thinking builds up the brain cells and keeps them in good condition.

The brain is the seat of consciousness. It is there that you say, "I am, I can, I will." It is there that you take your stand of authority and decree what your life shall be. From this throne room orders are sent to every cell in the body. No organ is more directly controlled by divine intelligence, more quickly responsive to it, or more readily healed.

Babies or children afflicted with any brain complication respond readily to the thought of divine intelligence, light, and order. The person who seeks to give help in any case of mental disturbance should diligently guard his own mind against confusion, doubt, or negation. He should fix his attention on

*Mind Renewal* 47

God, the source of light, joy, and harmony. Thus his own consciousness will remain elevated, dynamic with faith.

When a person keeps his mind renewed in Truth and his thoughts lifted Godward, he draws those who need healing up out of the darkness into the light of Truth.

Never think of those you would help as being mentally deficient or obsessed. Steadily know for them: *Divine intelligence is bathing every cell of your brain in healing light. Divine substance renews and restores it. Divine order is established in your mind. You are illumined. You are growing in the light of God.*

Persons who have not pursued and established some constructive line of thinking in their minds are inclined as they grow older to let their thoughts run in timeworn ruts. God, Divine Mind, the supreme intelligence planning and controlling all things, has provided us with sufficient mental food to last throughout eternity. There is not nor will there ever be a dearth of helpful, upbuilding things to think about.

Keep your brain cells replenished with new, living thoughts. Bless them with this word: *You are built up and sustained in the living substance of Divine Mind. You are the instrument of divine intelligence and wisdom. Through you the thoughts of God come to me. Daily God is blessing you with new life, new substance, new inspiration. You are full of light, blessed by renewing power. I consecrate my brain to God and give thanks for its perfect functioning.*

Divine intelligence illumines you that you may see, know, and understand. Let the Christ light in. Through your willingness to accept the guidance of divine intelligence your thoughts become centered and poised in Truth. Released from ignorance, error, and misunderstanding, your mind feeds on God thoughts of faith, harmony, love, and joy. It is sound, sane, and strong. It cannot become darkened, weakened, or lost, for God is your light and intelligence.

# The Tree of Life

LIFE! LIFE! Eternal, harmonious life! This is the message the Christ imparts to you. Through your very own consciousness He speaks His word of wholeness. Within your body, His living temple, the light of divinity shines. A restorative stream of life and harmonizing peace flows along your spinal cord. Each nerve of your body is a messenger in the service of the Spirit of life.

Physically, the spine is considered the main support of the body, but in the light of Truth it is far more than that. It is the trunk of the tree of life, and by means of its branches—the nerves—the thoughts of the mind are carried to the body and the needs of the body are transmitted to the mind.

Be still and know that there is but one Mind over all, one intelligence in all and through all. Your thoughts are quickened in Divine Mind. They are alive and powerful. Keep them harmonious, fearless, and full of faith so that they may serve God's purpose only.

"I am the vine, ye are the branches." You cannot be separated from the life of God. No part of your body need be lacking in life and strength. The light of divine intelligence is shining clearly, clearly within you to reveal to you God's perfect life.

"I am the vine." Speak the words again and again. Know that your spinal cord is the trunk of the tree of life within you. In it the intelligent, directive life of God is embodied. You are supported by His strength. Your life is directed by divine intelligence. Out to every little nerve end, out to every tiny cell, into every muscle the current of God life is flowing.

Every nerve in your body is a branch going out from the tree of life. There is no obstruction to God's message of life, love, and power. Clearly, clearly the word of life and wholeness is conveyed to every part of your body. Into your limbs, your feet, your hands, your arms it flows, a quickening, life-giving, healing current.

Orderly renewal, adjustment, and restoration are now taking place. Every vertebra is perfectly aligned. No nerve is impinged on. Every one is a perfect instrument of life, carrying God's message of peace, strength, light, and wholeness.

May I ask you who read these words to unite with me in a prayer and affirmation of faith and blessing especially for those who have suffered from infantile paralysis? The minds of such persons need to be fed with positive thoughts of life. Those who care for them need to employ thoughts of faith, joy, strength, and wholeness; to consecrate hands, heart, and mind to the healing service of Him who said, "Suffer the little children . . . to come unto me."

## The Tree of Life

The gift of Jesus Christ is life more abundant. He has placed His healing gift in our hands, heart, and mind that we may use it in every service we render. Inner thoughts of blessing as well as outer service of hands impart His healing love.

With faith centered in the Saviour let us declare for those who need help: *Life more abundant quickens you now. By the power and authority of Jesus Christ every nerve and muscle in your body is vitalized, rebuilt, and restored. From within you the life of God flows freely to every cell and tissue. You are strong, you are joyous, you are free and unafraid. You are made whole.*

Spines can be straightened. Paralysis can be healed. Muscles can be restored and nerves repaired. It can be done. It has been done through faith in God. It is being done now.

# *God in Control*

THERE IS help, there is cure for the epileptic, as well as for any type of sufferer from spasms, fits, or fainting seizures in which consciousness and muscular, nerve, or emotional control is temporarily lost.

Pause here for a moment and declare for all who may suffer any such inharmonious experience: *God is in control. God is Spirit, good omnipotent. Apart from Him there is no overcoming power. God is life, love, peace, and purity. God's will now fulfilled in you is health.*

There can be no lapse of consciousness, no cessation of peaceful, orderly life in God. In Him is no darkness, no lack of control. Neither need there be in any one of His children.

In working with God for the healing of epilepsy or any similar appearance, we must lay hold of the Spirit of wholeness, acknowledge its presence, and call forth its intelligence and power in the consciousness of the one whom we would help.

Erratic, uncontrolled activity of the mental, physical, or emotional life can be corrected by realization of the truth that Jesus spoke "One is your master, *even* the Christ." Never for an instant give way to the thought that some subconscious condition is in

## God in Control

control. It was to such untrue ideas as these that Jesus said, "Come out of him."

Charles Fillmore has written: "The superconscious is ever ready to pour forth divine blessing, quick to respond to the call of the conscious, which it meets on the middle ground of the subconscious. Spirit is omnipresent, but man has hedged himself about by a world of illusion of his own creating, and through its mists he does not see the Father, or catch the light from the superconscious. Jesus came to give us conscious control of the intelligence and the power necessary to dispel these mists, in order that 'the true light, *even the light* which lighteth every man, coming into the world' might shine full upon us."

Any condition that causes a person to lose conscious control of himself is merely a mist, an illusion, a false sense of separation from the principle of life within him. It can be and is immediately dispelled when the clear-shining light of the Christ Mind, the glory of the Christ love and faith, is directed toward it.

If you have experienced attacks of unconsciousness put them behind you as a thing of the past and be no longer alarmed or afraid. Set about now in even the little things that come to you to establish self-control in your life, to let God's will, His law of order and harmony, be done in you and in every condition of your life. Give the good, the pure, and the true supremacy in your thoughts. Say to yourself frequently, *One is my master, even the Christ.*

Neither condemn yourself for previous indulgences that have been permitted in order to avoid any excitement or resistance of your will, nor permit them longer to remain with you. Give God, your good, control. Know the Truth and fearlessly apply it: *God is my perfect will. His will in me is perfection and wholeness.*

When the disciples of Jesus asked Him why they could not heal the boy who had so little control of himself that he fell into the fire or the water, Jesus answered, "Because of your little faith."

Never allow yourself to think, "This condition cannot be healed." The prayer of faith annuls every hopeless thought or verdict; the light of Truth pierces the mist of doubt and reveals the divinity, the Christ mastery of the inner spirit.

Affirm: *God's life is constant, unbroken, eternal. I am quickened in His consciousness of life. All sense of confusion or uncertainty has vanished. My thoughts are centered and poised in the Christ Mind. I am conscious of His constant power and strength sustaining me and I am healed.*

You have given God control. You are triumphant, you are free, you are made whole!

# *Relaxation*

IN THE functions of mind and body, in the life of all nature, we find rest and activity alternating, making up the rhythm of life in us and in our world.

Only in our thoughts do we become too tense to enter into the rhythmic swing of things that makes life easier for us. Physicians tell us not to be troubled when our mind, which we may have been using too strenuously in ways of stress, hurry, and worry, seems to go blank for a few seconds now and then. It is nothing to be alarmed about. It is just nature's provident way of providing rest and recuperation for the brain cells.

Perhaps the most helpful relaxation of all is that which we are able to enjoy even while we are actively engaged: the thought of peace that keeps us poised in love and understanding even when things are humming all around us; the awareness of God's protective, harmonizing love even when strident voices denounce us or danger seems imminent; the consciousness of His inflowing life even in the face of disease or death.

There is never a moment when some part of the body cannot enjoy perfect relaxation. It may be no more than a single finger or toe, but that relaxed portion is relaying peace to all the rest of the body. Practice relaxing even a small part of your body at a time, practice releasing one tense thought each day and prove what it will do for you.

Each day, if possible, it is a splendid practice to stop all physical activity for several short periods of communion with God, to rest even a few seconds in the consciousness of His inner presence in you, His omnipresence around you. Nothing in life is so blessed, so creative, so productive as those pregnant moments when you choose to realize, "Be still, and know that I am God."

Life, like a pendulum, swings rhythmically into the spiritual substance of God, gathering momentum from His Holy Spirit, and swinging back again into the physical life and world to distribute the substance gained for the upkeep of the outer man.

Seek to know, to rest in the universal rhythm that controls all motion, prevents stagnation, and adds grace and beauty to all that God has created. Enter into the harmony of living, and you will decrease the wear and tear on your body cells.

Never feel that relaxation is a difficult feat. It is natural to you. When you were an infant you could relax completely. Tenseness is unnatural; it is acquired only as you accumulate troubled thoughts. If you have possibly acquired a hurried, worried method of working, begin now to let go. Trust God more completely. Let Him do the work through

*Relaxation*

you, and your daily tasks will prove joyous, harmonious, successful, and remunerative. You can trust God to illumine you and direct you along paths of health, peace, and plenty. You can trust Him to heal and to sustain you in perfect health.

Absolute trust in God assures perfect relaxation. As you relax in the assurance of His almighty supervision and turn your face toward Him, every cell in your body faces His light. It becomes radiantly alive as it rests in a perfect current of life unobstructed by any tenseness. You also rest, in mind, body, and soul, not from sheer weariness but in fulfillment of the rhythmic renewal of the God life in the midst of you.

Take a prayer, such as *The Prayer of Faith,* by Hannah More Kohaus:

> "God is my help in every need;
> God does my every hunger feed;
> God walks beside me, guides my way
> Through every moment of the day.
>
> "I now am wise, I now am true,
> Patient, kind, and loving, too.
> All things I am, can do, and be,
> Through Christ, the Truth that is in me.
>
> "God is my health, I can't be sick;
> God is my strength, unfailing, quick;

God is my all, I know no fear,
Since God and love and Truth are here."

Adapt the varying phrases of the prayer to meet your different needs. No matter how busy you may be, you will experience no depletion, no letdown when you work knowing that you can do all things through Christ. Your body will not fear or manifest disease when you know that God is your health. Your mind will not become tense or confused as you realize that the source of all wisdom is within you.

Relaxation is not inaction. It is the perfect poise in Spirit that enables one to crest the waves of life composed, serene, joyous, and unafraid.

At the center of your being Christ abides. Let go, beloved, let go, and rest in the light of His inner presence. *You are quiet, you are poised, you are renewed in Him now.* All glory and praise be to Jesus Christ who abides in you.

# *Life-Sustaining Breath*

AT THE time of your birth, when you drew your first breath, your body began to function as an independent human being. Even so now, when you open your mind to the inspiration of the Holy Spirit, the light of Christ is directed into every cell of your body. It functions through your entire being. You are reborn in Christ and you become a new creature, radiantly, completely alive.

Your lungs were quickened by your initial breath. The lungs receive the indrawn breath and impart its life-renewing qualities to the blood. This is known as the external respiration, the oxygen being passed into the blood and the carbon dioxide taken from it. Then there is the internal respiration when the life-renewing exchange takes place between the blood and the body cells. Doesn't it make you feel thoroughly alive all over when you think of each tiny cell breathing in new life, letting go of the old?

The life-sustaining, temperature-controlling, revivifying air you breathe is readily associated in thought with God about you and within you as omnipresent Spirit, the perfect life that pervades your body and makes and keeps you whole and free.

You need fear no lung trouble. Let the light of

Truth that has illumined you reveal to you your perfect trachea, bronchial tubes, and lungs.

Life! Beautiful, wondrous, eternal life is God's gift to you. With every indrawn breath you breathe in life; with every outgoing breath you give it forth. Each respiration starts a fresh current of life flowing through your lungs, to every part of your body, so that you may be constantly renewed, nurtured, and built up in the perfect life of God.

With every inspiration of thought that comes to you, you appropriate something to God. With every outpouring of that inspiration, clothed in words or deeds of faith, love, life, and blessing you express God. Thus does God breathe through you the breath of His own Spirit and permeate you with His restorative, all-sustaining, ever-enduring life.

No croupy, asthmatic, or bronchial constriction, obstruction, or congestion can remain when you know that the breath of the Almighty is moving freely through you. You are not subject to climate. When you associate your breathing with the breath of God and know that His Holy Spirit of light, life, and freedom is active in you, nothing can retard the free flow of air through your lungs.

When children suffer from croup, seek in every way to free them from all thoughts of fear or depression. Make them as happy and free as a little child should always be. Fill their days with bright, constructive things and as you tuck them into bed

## Life-Sustaining Breath 61

at night assure them of God's love and care. Use this prayer: *God breathes the breath of life through you. You know no fear. You are free. You are whole.* Teach the child to say, *"God breathes through me. I am strong and free."*

Wherever you are always remember that God supplies the air you breathe. You are never shut away from His breath of life.

Keep your windows open, those of your mind as well as the windows of your home or workroom. Let in the clean, fresh air and new, health-creating ideas. Both are expressions of the breath, the inspiration of the Almighty. Do not let fears or fancies deprive you of the good, pure air that God has provided for you, or permit disbelief or prejudice to close your mind to the inspiration of Truth.

When you pray, whether it be the prayer of a few seconds or of a longer period of meditation, concentrate your faith on God and you will feel the life-renewing quickening of the divine breath.

This is a helpful thought to use:

*God breathes through me the breath of life. I am receptive to His life. Every cell in my body responds to Him. I am quickened, built up, and restored. The inspiration of the Almighty fills my mind. I am conscious of new life. I am unafraid. I am alive, wholly alive, gloriously alive in every part of my body!*

"Jehovah God formed man . . . and breathed

into his nostrils the breath of life." That breath has never been withdrawn. God breathes through you the breath of divine life and every cell of your body is radiant with life.

# Bless Your Heart

Y OUR HEART represents your inmost character, the radiant loveliness of your inner self, the divine ideals and aspirations that are known only to God and yourself.

Within you is the inner chamber, the holy of holies, where you commune with your Father in secret, where "spirit with Spirit can meet," and God speaks with you in the silence.

Upon your heart God has written His law of life, order, and harmony. Here you approach the city that "lieth foursquare," the four-dimensional realm signified by the four chambers of the heart. Here one comprehends the perfect consciousness of life, with spirit, soul, mind, and body in complete co-ordination and wholeness. Here the Christ indwelling, the beloved Son of God, has established His throne. In your heart His love is generated.

Just as the brain is considered the seat of thought and the lungs the center of the breath of life, so the heart is known as the center of love. The light of divine intelligence has quickened your mind. You may use it as limitlessly as you choose. The breath of the Almighty has given life to your lungs. You may appropriate His holy breath, His Spirit, in all that you do. So love, the mighty redeeming, adjusting power of God, the healing balm for every inharmony, radiates from your heart.

Love, light, and intelligence co-ordinated in you, bring the perfect life of God into manifestation in your life and world. Love, light, and inspiration on the spiritual plane, expressed as feeling, thought, and aspiration on the physical plane, have everything to do with your perfect development in spirit, soul, and body.

Bless your heart, even as Jesus blessed it for all time when He said, "Let not your heart be troubled, neither let it be fearful." Draw close to the healing Christ and be set free this very moment from uncertainty, pain, and fear.

Blessed is your heart. Through it flows the pure, renewing life and love of God, His peace and understanding. The wise Creator who set in motion the rhythmic order of the universe has caused His life and love to pulsate through your heart in perfect harmony. He has established a pause, a time of rest, in every heartbeat in order that perfect renewal may be steadily, quietly carried on.

Your heart cannot be troubled, disturbed, or diseased, or weakened, nor can it be worn out by age, as long as you realize that it is a living center through which the love of God flows to bless you eternally, to keep your life harmonious, to pour forth through you to others a healing benediction.

When you remember that wherever you are

*Bless Your Heart*

God's love and life is functioning through you the effect of high altitude on the heart action will be corrected. Divine love is not lessened nor its power decreased one whit whether you are on the high mountain peak or in the lowlands.

Ascend the mountains with this thought in mind:

*I am lifted up unto the unchanging life and love of God. My heart is controlled by divine love and understanding. It is strong and fearless. Its action is steady and true.*

Let your heart feel after God. It will do this naturally if you do not entertain any thoughts of depression, doubt, bitterness, or fear. Let the feeling of good will, courage, and peace that is sustained in your heart by Jesus Christ be accompanied by thoughts of faith and rejoicing as you bless your heart in His name with living words of Truth:

*Blessed is my heart. The pure love and life of God pulsate through it in perfect rhythm and order. It is cleansed of all misunderstanding, inharmony, impurity, and disease. It is free, confident, and unburdened. Its action is well ordered and harmonious. Its perfection is established. I rest in the assurance that Jesus Christ is always with me. His peace and faith infold me. My heart is untroubled and unafraid. It is perfected in His love.*

# Alive to Your Finger Tips

WOULD YOU know just how closely, how intimately your life is linked with the invigorating life of God? Then consider the vascular system of your body. The blood conveying life and sustenance to every cell goes out from your heart through the arterial branches until it reaches the capillaries that connect the smallest arteries with the smallest veins: then it flows back again to the heart.

In another lesson we shall consider the arteries and the veins, but today we are going to think about the capillaries, the most minute channels of the blood stream. The walls of the capillaries consist of one layer of endothelial cells continuous with the layer that lines the arteries, the veins, and the heart. There is no separation, no rift in the channels that carry the blood stream of life through the body, neither is there any dissimilarity between the cells that make up the capillaries and the cells that line the heart.

Hold your finger up before you. Look through it toward the light. See the pink glow of life in its tip. It is your faithful capillaries that have carried the blood to the surface. It would take you a long time to count them even in a single finger tip and

## Alive to Your Finger Tips

yet they are a very important part of the blood-conveying system in your body.

Should you ever feel that your life is far removed from the life of God, whose Spirit is the great heart of the universe, just hold your hand up to the light and let those little capillaries that seem so remote from your heart and yet are so important to the life of your body, be an object lesson to you. Remember that each one bears in its formation the same kind of tissue that lines the heart.

Should you ever think that your life is of no importance and that the world would be as well off without you, just consider the function of these tiny capillaries. We are told that "in the glandular organs the capillaries supply the substances requisite for secretion; in the alimentary canal they take up some of the elements of digested food; in the lungs they absorb oxygen and give up carbon dioxide; in the kidneys they discharge the waste products collected from other parts; all the time, everywhere through their walls, that interchange is going on which is essential to the life of the whole body.

Although the capillaries are exceedingly minute in themselves, it is in them that the chief work of the blood is done. In like manner it is in humanity, in you and through your life, that the chief work of the Father is carried on. You have a part and place in the divine scheme of life. You are the image and likeness of your Creator.

Within your capillaries a continual process of giving and receiving is carried on. The health of your body is dependent on this interchange. Within the life of humanity, within your life as an individual, there is likewise established a system of giving and receiving between God and you, between you and the universal Christ body, between you and other persons. As an individual you are peculiarly well fitted to carry on a certain life-distributing service. It may be done through the love you feel toward others, the work you do each day, the thoughts you think, the joy you share, or the home you provide.

God's life flows ceaselessly out through your life and your life flows ceaselessly back to Him where it is renewed, refreshed, and restored to its spiritual purity and purpose. Acknowledge and accept your God-given portion of life, saying:

*Straight from the heart of the Infinite the life of God flows to me in a ceaseless stream. My circulation is perfect. I am a channel for His free-flowing life. There is a constant interchange of life, love, and harmony between God and me, between me and other persons. Freely, gladly, I receive; fearlessly, joyously, I give. I am aglow with the perfect life of God.*

# Rhythmic Arterial Life

STEADILY, *rhythmically the life of God pulses through my body.*

This is the message that your arteries bear to you as moment by moment, second by second, your blood courses through them. Let your finger rest gently on wrist or temple and feel the tap, tap, tap of your pulse. It denotes your ever-renewing life.

Your arteries do not have to make some great effort to get the blood to come into them. It is propelled into them from your heart, carried along them by a divinely perfected muscular action. In the same way the life of God is propelled through you to keep you alive, strong, and well. You are one with the perfect life of God.

God is life and God also is love. At the center of all things the infinite heart of the Creator constantly sends forth life. The pulsing power of divine love propels it. The beating of your heart, the throb of your pulse against your finger bears witness to it. The incoming and outgoing ocean tide, the rise and fall of waves upon the shore bear witness to it, the march of the stars in their orbits, the turning of the earth upon which we live, the recurrent seasons, the dawn of each day, the regular return of the night—these and countless other things testify of the steadily pulsing life of God that is propelled by the almighty power of the Creator in and through all things.

Your heart does not wait for your arteries to draw upon it before it replenishes them with the reoxygenized blood that means life to the various members of your body. No; steadily, quietly it beats, regularly, rhythmically it forces the life stream into the arteries.

God does not wait for you to implore Him for life. Constantly and in divine order He pours His ever-renewing life, love, and strength in and through you. Every throb of your heart reminds you of the pulsing life of God, tells you of your oneness with that life and your right and freedom to use it.

God's life is ageless, deathless, abiding. Your life in Him is likewise ageless, deathless, abiding. In order that your arteries may bear witness to God's eternal life, bless them daily with thoughts of the renewal and resiliency of life. Keep your mind replenished with thoughts of life and Truth, love and good will, joy and tenderness. Let the knowledge of your daily growth in Christ replace any possible old-age thoughts.

A very earnest Truth student once said to me, "I am not seeking renewal of youth. I want the experience, the maturity of life. I want to mature in Christ, His wisdom, love, faith, and power."

Without fully realizing it this friend has found

## Rhythmic Arterial Life

the keynote of eternal life, the secret of eternal progress, the formula of eternal body renewal. No thinking person desires to retain the inexperience of youth, or to go back to it. He wants to mature, but he would carry forward with him into his maturity the buoyancy of youthful life, the zest of living, the joy of conquest, the prophecy of hope, the assurance of faith, and greatest of all, an increasing consciousness of love. It is right that he should.

Now with the thought of maturity in Christ uppermost in your mind bless your arteries, saying:

*Father, I thank Thee for the gift of life, for its unretarded, rhythmic flow through every artery in my body. Strong, steady, deathless, it pulsates through me, bearing to every part of my body Thy assurance of love, wisdom, and wholeness. I now surrender every personal doubt, fear, hard feeling, and shortcoming that would deny or retard the perfect flow of Thy life or love. I am now open and receptive to Thee. I am putting on the new man, taking on the character of Christ. I am wholly alive, safely alive, eternally alive in Thee. Fearlessly I go forward to my perfect maturity in Truth. Father, I thank Thee for the gift of life.*

You are blessed with life, ageless, resilient, perfect life. Praise God!

# The Circuit of Life

WE TAKE our torch of faith and go to the various organs and parts of our body to instruct and bless them with the light of Truth and wholeness, and in return they teach us many priceless lessons. We learn from them of coordination and perfect obedience. We marvel at the blending of all the cells and functions of the body in the common purpose of maintaining the whole. Each and every part of the body teaches us something of our close relationship to God.

From our arteries we learn how the lifeblood is constantly propelled through our body. From our veins we learn a lesson perhaps not quite so familiar to us but most precious nevertheless. It concerns the orderly way in which our life is constantly returned to the source of life for purification and renewal.

From the heart the blood flows out through the arteries into the tiny capillaries that bridge across from artery to vein, and back to the heart. Then it is carried into the lungs where it is renewed by the air we breathe.

From the heart of the Infinite the life of God flows into us, crosses by the tiny bridgeways of our daily life and affairs, and flows back again to

## The Circuit of Life

Him by whom our mistakes are smoothed out, our diseases healed, our iniquities forgiven. New inspiration is given to us through the breath of the Almighty.

When we meditate on the way in which our life returns to God for restoration as regularly and surely as it flows into us from Him, the function of the veins of the body becomes closely related to His all-redeeming system of grace.

We all know how the blood flows back to the heart through the veins. It is not propelled by a throbbing life force but gently urged onward in the right direction, protected against any backward flow by little valves, and as gently drawn into the heart by a slight suction.

Does this not outpicture the way God draws our life constantly into the circle of His restorative love, where it is lifted up into the light of His divine inspiration to renew us in understanding and wisdom, to nuture us in faith and love. "I have loved thee with an everlasting love: therefore with lovingkindness have I drawn thee."

Doesn't that take the fear and the misunderstanding out of life? We carry many things into maturity that we do not need to bear. Sometimes life gets all congested and clogged up with them, and it seems hard for us to move along. We may long for the assurance of forgiveness and yet feel that it is denied us, all because we have not understood how ceaselessly our life is flowing back to God, how constantly He forgives, how continuously He restores.

Let us think for just a moment about the meaning of forgiveness, God's forgiveness of us, our forgiveness of others and of ourselves. Let us turn the word "forgive" around and look at it from another angle: "give for." This simplifies and clarifies its meaning and is exactly what God does and what we do when we forgive.

Jesus "forgave" the palsied man. He gave him wholeness for sickness. God "forgives" our mistakes and shortcomings. He gives us love to replace our animosities, active words to replace idle ones, understanding to replace ignorance. God gives the things needed to perfect our expression of life in the place of the mortal thoughts, things, and desires that tend toward destruction or stagnation.

When the venous blood reaches the lungs, carbon dioxide is replaced by oxygen, which is the breath of life to the body. We breathe forth the carbon dioxide, and it becomes life to growing plants. Nothing is wasted in the orderly expression of life. So when you keep the channel of prayer and thought clear and open toward God, your life flows in ceaseless praise and understanding to Him. If there is aught that needs adjustment, it is clarified and cleansed. God replaces any insufficiency with His all-sufficiency, and you are built up anew.

## The Circuit of Life

Now let us be still and know that God has provided a divine channel that is ever open and clear for the constant return of our life to Him in order that we may be hourly, momently renewed, forgiven if need be, and restored. It is the channel of divine grace. We need hold no sin against ourselves and we must never hold any sin or shortcoming against another by intolerance, misunderstanding, or condemnation.

Remember, the venous circulation is just as important as the arterial. Bless your veins with this thought:

*I rejoice in the knowledge that my life is constantly flowing out from the light and life of God, and being drawn back to Him for purification and renewal by His almighty love for me. A perfect equilibrium exists in my life, work, and affairs. I forgive freely, and am forgiven. I am loving and kind toward all people because God is loving and kind toward me. There is no obstruction, no barrier anywhere in my mind, veins, or affairs. I am peaceful and harmonious. I am free, unafraid, whole, and well.*

"If thou return to the Almighty, thou shalt be built up."

# Blood of the Covenant

THERE IS no greater degree of intelligence shown in any part of your body, or in any part of the universe for that matter, than that which is displayed in one tiny drop of your blood. There is no more ceaseless or orderly activity carried on anywhere.

The words *blood* and *life* are often used interchangeably. It is logical that they should be, for in the blood we find all the constituents of life, and in the activities of life we find the same interchange and intercommunion that is carried on within the body by the blood.

Let us consider the functions of the blood. First of all we know that it carries oxygen, the very elixir of life, from the lungs to every cell in the body. Have you ever stood on the summit of a high hill in the sunlight and breathed deeply of the clear, tonic air? Did you feel new life run tingling through every part of your body until you seemed light, free, gloriously alive? Your blood, refreshed by abundant oxygen, was coursing through your veins, carrying the light, joy, and substance of life to every part of your body.

To me the blood is the most interesting part of the body. I like to think of those little corpuscles,

*Blood of the Covenant* 77

so flexible and elastic that they can make their way through the tissues in openings smaller than themselves, and then resume their original shape. Some way I sense that that is how God comes into our body temple. He has made His Spirit adaptable to our use. Infinite, limitless, universal, omnipresent is our God, and yet He comes into our finite life and there resumes His perfection, His original beauty and glory. Those whose eyes are quickened in the light of Truth exclaim, "I behold the Christ in you."

One there was whom we love, who knew the transmuting power of the blood. One there was who loved us with an eternal love, who gave His life, His blood, to us that He might become the very life of our being. Never has any blood transfusion performed by man approached the marvel of this gift of Jesus to us.

Without doubt He knew that the essence of life is embodied in every drop of blood. He understood how the blood nourishes the body, how it is equipped to defend the body, how it constantly bathes the body in a purifying stream of life. In no other manner could Jesus have made His life more real and available to us that He did when He blessed the sacrament of life, saying, "This is my blood of the covenant."

The blood renders to us the greatest possible service in distributing nutriment through our body, and an equal service in picking up waste material and carrying it to the lungs, kidneys, bowels, or skin for elimination. We are not left defenseless against infection or disease. We rejoice in good red blood, for it denotes vigor, strength, and vitality, but we should not overlook or fail to be thankful for the white blood corpuscles that protect the body and defend it against infection.

You could no more count the cells in your body than you could count the stars in the heavens. Yet every cell must be supplied with the things needed to enable it to do its work. It must be protected against the invasion of disease and relieved of waste material. Think of the intelligence of your blood, which carries on this work so efficiently that you are unaware of it.

"This is my blood of the covenant." What is the covenant of God with you, with all people? It is the covenant of life, love, peace, and order. It is the pledge of substance, wholeness, and harmony. It is the assurance of light, faith, and inspiration.

How does the blood, the spiritual essence of the life of Jesus Christ, affect you? It feeds your mind with living words, builds up your awareness of God, and nourishes every cell in your body with the substance of the perfect Christ body. It defends you against destructive thoughts and impulses, and relieves you of your shortcomings, your burdens, or aught else that needs elimination from your life.

Jesus invites you: "Come unto me." For building

up and enriching the blood, for purifying any blood disorder, or correcting any disturbance of the flow, be still and know:

*This is my blood of the covenant, God's covenant of life, wholeness, freedom, and purity. It is bearing His living substance to every cell in my body, washing away every impurity, regenerating me with the pure life of Christ.*

"The blood of Jesus his Son cleanseth us from all sin."

# Commune with Your Lord

LET EVERY outer thought be still. Let every desire be purified. Let every cell in your body temple reflect the light of the divine presence.
"*The Lord is in His holy temple,
Let earth before Him silence keep.*"

Within you His perfect work is being done. Silently, without sound of hammer, the Son of God is erecting His perfect temple of life and wholeness. He is resurrecting you to newness of life and understanding.

Gently, lovingly the living word is being impressed on your mind. New light, new inspiration is shining into your consciousness. You are being quickened, beloved, you are being quickened now into the likeness of Jesus Christ, the beloved Son of God.

*Jesus Christ is now with you raising you to His consciousness of wholeness.*

*Jesus Christ is now with you raising you to His consciousness of peace.*

Let the burdens fall from your shoulders.
Let anxiety drop from your mind.
Let fear slip away from your heart.
Let the outer affairs be released.
Let every shackle be loosed.

The Lord is in His holy temple. He is making every wise and true adjustment. He is forgiving every iniquity, healing every disease. He is harmonizing every discord, supplying every need.

Enshrined within your soul, Spirit of your spirit, the Christ indwelling is communing with you now. To your lips He has lifted the cup of His redeemed life. He is feeding you now with the bread of life, nurturing your soul with His love and substance, renewing your body in strength and wholeness.

While you are communing with the Christ, partaking of His life, love, and substance in the stillness of the inner temple of your body, He is pouring out upon your affairs the blessing of His Holy Spirit. His wisdom, judgment, and justice are being meted out in all that pertains to your life, service, supply, or environment.

The Lord is in His holy temple. *Listen.* To you is His assurance given. "Be of good cheer; thy faith hath made thee whole."

## The Mediator

ALTHOUGH I was but a young girl when I was baptized, from that time on Jesus Christ became an ever-present baptismal fount to me. I could instantly be immersed in Him when my thoughts, feelings, or desires needed cleansing, controlling, or uplifting. He was as the river of life flowing out from the throne of God. I could rest by that river and gain peace and poise in mind and body. I could bathe in its cleansing current and gain forgiveness. I could partake of its refreshing waters and be restored.

In those days God seemed vast and incomprehensible to me. He was like a mighty ocean of power, and I was afraid of Him, but there was no thought of fear in connection with Jesus Christ. When I thought of Him as a person it was as the Healer of Galilee who, surrounded by milling throngs, took little children in His arms and blessed them. In Spirit He was the clear, sparkling stream of life that the Psalmist described.

Paul's description of Jesus Christ as the mediator has always been most precious to me. The river running through the pasture land is the intermediary between the uncontrolled waterfall up in the hills where the stream has its origin, and the ocean

## The Mediator

with waves mountain high, where it attains its ultimate power.

One day I was meditating on Jesus Christ as the Mediator, thinking of Him as the stream of life, when there came clearly to my mind the thought of the action and purpose of the lymphatic vascular system. The blood, being contained in a set of closed vessels—arteries and veins—does not come into direct contact with the cells of the body, except those which line the walls of the blood vessels. Therefore a medium of exchange between the blood and the cells of the body is necessary. A fluid known as lymph serves this purpose.

Lymph bathes all portions of the body not directly reached by the blood, protects the vital organs, cushions the joints. It takes to each cell the material it needs for its functional activity. Also it picks up and returns to the blood the products of fuctional activity. These may be simple waste or some substance capable of being used by some other tissue. Lymph acts as an intermediary between the blood and the tissues.

The lymphatics are the channels through which the lymph is carried back to the blood, thus preventing any stagnation of fluid in the tissues. In structure and arrangement they resemble the veins. Tiny lymph nodes, each with an inner structure resembling a sponge, are placed along the course of the lymphatics and grouped in protective chains near the great blood vessels. They serve as filters and as a defense against infection.

Many cells are far from the source of supply and the organs of elimination. Therefore a medium is needed to distribute supplies and dispose of waste. This need is met by the blood and the lymph.

In cases of blood poisoning or of any disturbance that causes the glands or lymph nodes to become inflamed or tender—at any time when infection of any nature sends out its warning signals—think of the stream of pure life flowing out from the source of life within you. Step into the current and be made whole. Rest by the refreshing stream that runs through the pasture land of spiritual thought and prayer and be restored.

Consider the work done for you by your lymphatic system. Think also of the work carried on by the Christ who abides in you. Patiently, silently, wisely He works with you to bring into your mind and life the thoughts and gifts of God that nourish the inner man. At the same time He relieves you of undesirable accretions or conditions. Sometimes even the things that seemed wasted in your life are converted into valuable assets.

The work of Christ within you is dependent on one thing only. That is your willingness to yield to the perfect interchange and blending of His nature with yours. He is the mediator between you and the Godhead, the stream of life and love that flows

## The Mediator

through your life bearing into it all that is eternal and divinely good, carrying out of it all that would be burdensome or detrimental to you. His activity in you and your reciprocation of His service means perfection for you and blessing for all who come in contact with you. Affirm:

*Every cell in my body is bathed in the pure stream of Christ life and love. Every thought is cleansed and redeemed. I now let go of fear, error, passion, death, disease. They are washed away by the redeeming life of Jesus Christ. New life, new strength, the unfailing power of divine wholeness now flow through me. Every cell in my body is pure, clean, and perfect. I step into the current and I am made whole. Praise God.*

# A Faithful Servant

YOUR STOMACH is a discerning and faithful servant, also a responsible and responsive one. Through the large nerve centers controlling it it is very closely associated with your mind and your heart. No organ in your body is more quickly affected by moods.

Love is a great solvent, cheer a wonderful digestant, faith a perfect aid to assimilation. When love sends its cheering message of faith into your organism, the nerves controlling your stomach are immediately quickened and the process of digestion is carried on speedily and in order.

It may seem old-fashioned to say grace before meals, but you will find that as you practice putting aside all thought of burdens, worry, haste, distrust, dislike, and anger three times a day, and lifting your thoughts to God in love and gratitude, you will experience no stomach trouble. Each mealtime will prove an occasion on which not only your physical hunger is appeased but your soul is nourished by the living bread of Christ.

When you render thanks to God you are lifted up into the free grace of His Spirit. Mental congestion is relieved. Your mind is free to assist your stomach, to give thought to the food you eat, to

## A Faithful Servant

choose it wisely, eat it slowly, and enjoy it thoroughly.

Please do not think that when I advocate saying grace I mean dropping into a state of mental solemnity and uttering a few words by rote. When I approach a meal I thank God for His provision of food for all people. I praise Him within my heart, seldom aloud—which is a matter for each one to decide—for something happy, beautiful, or inspiring that has come to me between meals. Try it. If your experience is as mine has been, there will never be a time when you will not have something new, fresh, and uplifting to thank God for. It will surprise you how your perception and appreciation will increase.

Never carry financial worries to the table with you. Make it your business to let your mind be enriched by the substance of uplifting, upbuilding thoughts during meal hours. Thus as your stomach works to prepare the usable substance of your food for assimilation, your mind will work in harmony with it and lay hold of the substance of divine wisdom. Each meal will act as a prosperity treatment to increase your substance. You will leave the table fortified in mind, strengthened in body, happy in heart, prepared to succeed—and you will succeed.

As you eat your food, remember it is the fruit of someone's labor. Each slice of bread brings you the golden bounty of wheat fields. Each vegetable first graced someone's garden. The fruit drank in the sunshine, reveled in the rain, danced in the wind.

Let the peace of quiet acres, the bounty of grain fields, the loveliness of growing gardens, the beauty of yielding orchards, bless you as you eat. You may eat your meals in a crowded city restaurant, but they bring you the blessing of the great out-of-doors.

It is not mere eatables that the Father has supplied you with, something gross for the filling of your stomach. It is living substance, blessed and filled with joy, harmony, sunshine, life, and loveliness.

*Thank You, God, for perfect food for my mind and my body. Thank You for the power of discrimination, for the ability to choose my food wisely, to eat it with gladness, to digest it perfectly. Thank You for the substance of Your Spirit that has renewed my mind, established divine order in my stomach, and restored me to wholeness.*

# *Perfect Nutrition*

THE PERFECTLY nourished body is neither heavy and cumbersome with excess flesh nor is it emaciated, thin, and weak. The perfectly nourished body houses a well-nourished mind.

The image of God is implanted within you. You bring forth the Christ in perfection in your mind, body, and soul through daily living in conformity with Truth.

All souls do not grow by the same spiritual food, as is proved by the various teachings of different denominations. What may seem most essential to the religious life and growth of one person will leave another cold and uncomprehending.

As it is with the soul, so it is with the body. Food peculiarly adapted to one person's need will not meet the requirements of another. Diets especially helpful to one person may prove ineffectual or harmful to another.

Instinctively a normal, healthy appetite will call for the things most needed by the body. Your body knows what it needs. Every organ, every gland in your body is intelligent. If you have allowed your appetite to become unruly, making demands for an excessive amount of food, or to become pernickety so that much essential food is rejected, take your appetite in hand. Train and master it. As you regulate your desire for food, you will also regulate many thoughts in your mind that have to do with the maintenance of your perfect body.

Just as fruits, grains, vegetables, and nuts come to you laden with the substance they have drawn from moisture, sunshine, and soil, so the thoughts of Truth developed in your mind bring you the substance of divine light, wisdom, and power.

A person who is always craving something to eat, something to drink, something to smoke, something exciting to do, undoubtedly has a soul hunger that needs attention. When he is satisfied in spirit, he does not crave outer things constantly.

Worry, fear, nagging, any depleting or destructive thought habit wears a body down to abnormal thinness. A person whose taste has been diverted to foods that carry little nutriment, or who does not properly assimilate the food he eats, needs to take time each day for quiet relaxation and meditation when he definitely feeds his spirit, mind, and body with thoughts of peace, order, and substance and gives himself a chance to appropriate them.

By running and playing out of doors, children build up healthy appetites and sturdy bodies. Adults should not overlook the fact that a certain amount of outdoor recreation is likewise good for them. Frequently such aids to health as exercise, fresh air, and relaxation are overlooked. Forgotten, neglected,

## Perfect Nutrition

and unappreciated, these blessings surround man while he resorts to all kinds of expensive and often distasteful remedies.

If you turn to Him, God will help you to regulate your appetite, food, and mode of living so that all that pertains to you will be in perfect harmony and your body will take on the symmetry and beauty of the perfect pattern.

It is your privilege, your responsibility to feed and care aright for your mind, body, and soul. Watch your thoughts. Thoughts that make you nervous, crabbed, gloomy, angry, distrustful, or discontented are unsuitable food for your mind. They sap it of every worth-while idea. Watch your appetite and your tastes. Naturally, normally you will want and like the things that are right and good for your body.

Too much of anything becomes burdensome. If you have too much weight, eat too much food, and are trying to accumulate too many things, practice daily letting go of some surplus. Bless your body and your affairs with this affirmation:

*I lay aside every weight. I let go of all surplus. I share my all with God. He blesses my desires, my appetite, my food. He enables me to build and maintain a light, free, energetic body.*

Lack causes anxiety. Too much zeal and ambition use up energy and substance faster than they are acquired. Restlessness, dissatisfaction with life, or drastic economy trend to rob both mind and body of substance. If you are too thin and have insufficient strength, use this affirmation:

*God is my supply. I partake of His substance freely. There is no lack in my mind, body, or affairs. God quickens my appetite, and I eat, enjoy, and assimilate my food in divine order and harmony. He blesses my substance. There is abundance. I am perfectly nourished and provided for. My mind, body, and affairs are built up in the eternal substance of Being.*

# *Your Intelligent Liver*

THERE IS no laboratory in the world where a greater or more painstaking work is done than that which is carried on within your liver. It is helpful for you to know something of the functions of your body in order that you may work intelligently with them instead of thoughtlessly working against them.

Have you ever joyously thought of your liver in terms of appreciation for the good work that it does for you? It is a tireless worker. It is constantly abstracting certain materials from the blood and converting them into new substance that can be appropriated by the body for its upbuilding or eliminated from it when its purpose has been accomplished.

With the precision of a well-trained mathematician the liver stores up food properties needed by the body and pours them into the blood stream according to the demand for them. Functioning in conjunction with the other digestive organs, it has much to do with the maintenance of the equilibrium of the body as well as with the orderly, balanced distribution of rations for the cells.

When the liver is not functioning properly, dizziness is frequently experienced, and the stomach rejects food. Persons who suffer from travel sickness should hold steadfastly to the inner realization of perfect poise in Christ. When arranging for a journey, especially if it be on the ocean, it is good judgment to avoid any excessive indulgences that might unduly tax the digestive organs, particularly the liver.

Vitally connected with the stomach, spleen, pancreas, and intestines by the portal system of circulation, the liver is closely aligned in thought with the five-sense man and his material needs and desires. However, being divided into four lobes, it also directs our attention to the four-dimensional realm, the true spiritual estate of man.

"Portal" means door or gateway. When we think of the portal duct, which is the channel through which the blood enters the liver from the other digestive organs, we are reminded of the words of Jesus, "I am the door." Just as the function of the liver is protective and purifying for the life stream that passes through the portal duct, so the work of the Christ indwelling is protective, redemptive, and regenerative.

It is claimed that no organ in the body is more quickly regenerated. Therefore, we know that none is more responsive to Truth or more easily and readily healed when a person is willing to enter the portal of spiritual consciousness: the inner door or Christ way that leads to peace, poise, balance, wholeness.

The bile is an excretory medium for toxins and

metals. When one experiences inharmony from jaundice or gallstone trouble he should immediately free his mind from any hard, retarding, embittered thoughts, and definitely, constantly know that God who created the body temple is working with him to forgive, purify, and re-establish it in divine order and harmony.

Just as your liver can convert certain substances into building material for your body, so your mind, inspired by the Christ indwelling, can convert inharmonious thoughts into new ideas that convey the healing, freeing, cleansing love and faith of God to any part of the body and rebuild and restore it to order and perfection.

No hardening of the liver can take place, no cancer of this wonderful gland can take root or remain when the thoughts are centered in the directive love and wisdom of Christ. When we forgive ourselves and others and free our mind from misjudgment, bitterness, injustice, intolerance, and revenge, the liver and every organ of the body benefit. The consciousness is opened to the Christ light of life, and the body made accessible and receptive to the healing ray of divine love. Exultantly mind, heart, and body work together as the healing word is spoken:

*The redeeming love of God restores and regenerates me. Every cell in my liver is renewed by His power. I am healed, praise God, I am healed.*

Let every unpleasant experience be erased from your memory. Let every tense, fearful, hard thought be released from your mind. Your attention has been directed to the healing love of Jesus Christ. He has come into your life to free you from pain and suffering.

For jaundice or gallstones affirm:

*By the power of Jesus Christ every passageway of my body is clear, every function harmonious, every organ vitalized and restored.*

Let the generous loving-kindness of God fill you now as you bless your fellow men. Know that none is cowardly in Truth. None is greedy, lustful, hard, or merciless. When your blessing lovingly given to others returns to you, as it surely will, you will find that your world has changed. It will be peopled with friends. Everything without and within carries a blessing of love, unity, and wholeness to your body temple.

# *Perfect Elimination*

COME LET us be free. Let us willingly release the thoughts or things that clutter up our life. Let us open the door of our consciousness to the more abundant life of Jesus Christ and let it flow freely through us, a cleansing stream that purifies and redeems every organ, cell, and function in our body.

Every smallest part of our body organism teaches us a lesson of life, order, co-ordination, rhythm, and harmony. God has promised, "I will put my law in their inward parts, and in their heart will I write it." God has done His part. The law of divine order and wholeness is established in you. There is that which is akin to the divine in the fearlessness and intelligence of the organs in your body, the way they receive their sustenance and let go of all that is not needed.

There is no stagnation in the healthy body. Its perfect system of assimilation and elimination is unequaled by any invention of man. Life would be short indeed if the lungs were to hoard the air that is drawn into them, if the heart refused to release the blood for circulation through the body, or the stomach did not let go of food. We may well praise God for the wonderful manner in which every bodily function works for the good of the entire body. There is no grasping sense of possession. Even the smallest cell receives from the blood the properties it needs for its upbuilding and releases that which is no longer usable. A continual process of construction and purification is thus carried on.

Truly here is a lesson for us to learn: to let go of all thoughts that are a hindrance to us, and to accept and use the ones that draw us closer to God and give us peace of mind and health of body. Worried, impure, tense thoughts cause us to hold on to many untoward conditions in body and environment. Neglecting the inner urge that bids us let go of the old and make room for the new clogs our life with the debris of past mistakes, disappointments, and sufferings.

No function of the body teaches this lesson more clearly than the bowels. Constipation is most frequently a habit of neglect. People are too busy or too interested in other things to heed the call of nature, just as they are too concerned about the inharmony that may be troubling them to heed the call of faith and freedom.

"Ye shall know the truth, and the truth shall make you free." This is no idle promise. Truth frees your mind from ignorance, superstition, fear. It frees your body from inharmony and disease. It frees your character of undesirable traits. It frees you from the bond of unhappy memories and personal

## Perfect Elimination

inhibitions or limitations. Truth feeds your mind with living thoughts and quickens in you the more abundant life that Jesus promised.

Constipation, appendicitis, intestinal irritation, or rectal trouble will be quickly and permanently cured if you will take time at a regular hour every day to let go of the old and lay hold of the new. Let go of unwise cravings of the appetite, let go of characteristics that are not beneficial to yourself or others, let go of doubt, worry, condemnation, and fear.

Especially let go of the intolerant attitude, the merciless judgment that would mete out punishment for others, the "worm-of-the-dust" thoughts that are unworthy of you. The word vermiform means wormlike. The vermiform appendix is a narrow wormlike tube.

Just as merciful, spiritual thoughts lift up and free the mind, so fruit, the sun-ripened food that in the diet is the counterpart of spiritual thoughts, helps to keep the intestinal tract clear and clean. The child that from babyhood is taught regular habits of elimination and whose bowels are stimulated to action by a healthful mixture of fruit or fruit juices in his diet, seldom is troubled with appendicitis. The bowels are the seat of compassion and mercy. Teach the children to be merciful to every living thing. The humane vegetarian diet is especially helpful not only as a hamonizer for the digestive tract but also as a practical way of putting mercy into daily practice.

Release all worm-of-the-dust thoughts from your mind. Take on the Son-of-God ideas. The sun of righteousness has risen upon you "with healing in its wings."

Heed the call of the Christ to come up higher, to know the Truth and be set free. Heed His message of mercy, compassion, loving-kindness, and life more abundant. Heed His assurance that day by day, an all-loving Father provides for you. Daily declare:

*I now let go of every hindering, binding thought or desire. My mind and my body are open and receptive to the abundant life of Christ. It blesses me now with strength and freedom. I am cleansed. I am free. I am compassionate, unburdened, unhurried, unafraid. I am healed.*

# Abiding Strength

GOD IS your perfect strength. In Him is no weakness whatever. In Him you are strong, unafraid, perfect. Even as your body becomes radiant with life and strength when you recoginze it as the temple of God, so every cell becomes animated with new energy and vitality when you behold it lifted up into the light and wholeness of Spirit.

There are no weak spots in the perfect body God planned for you, no broken walls, no rupture.

In olden days almost the first thought directed toward a newborn baby was fear that the little one might become ruptured. Tortuous bands were applied that restricted circulation and intestinal action. Little muscles, tightly bound, became weakened. Now through understanding care of the infant, hernia has been greatly decreased. Mothers are coming to know that they must not surround their children with fear thoughts of weakness but must guide them in the right use of their strength instead of teaching them that certain portions of the abdominal walls or muscles are weak spots in the body. Bless the baby with a thought like this:

*God is your perfect strength. Every muscle and tissue in your body is strongly knit together into a perfect whole. His life vitalizes each organ and intestine. His intelligence keeps each part of the body adjusted and in its right place.*

Many adults have grown up with a great dread of hernia in their minds. This very fear is a recognition of weakness that is detrimental to the body cells and depressing to the muscles.

It is an established fact that man frequently becomes a superman in strength when on the spur of the moment he has some critical emergency to meet. Undreamed-of physical power rises up within him. In perfect co-ordination every muscle in his body responds to the demand with amazing results. This proves that the directive intelligence within man will work perfectly for him when it is unhampered by thoughts of depression, inability, and weakness.

As surely as a person considers some spot in his body as naturally weak and tries in all ways to save it from strain, just as surely does he tense the muscles in that part and throw undue strain on it in every effort he exerts.

Paul tells us how Abraham, by faith in the strength that came to him through divine inspiration, overcame even the infirmities of age. "Without being weakened in faith he considered his own body now as good as dead (he being about a hundred years old) . . . yet, looking unto the promise of God, he wavered not through unbelief, but waxed strong through faith, giving glory to God."

*Abiding Strength*

The promise is "They that wait for Jehovah shall renew their strength."

Train every cell in your body to know the strength of Jehovah. Train every muscle and nerve to wait on Him, to look to Him, to depend on Him for renewed strength. Train your mind in a steadfast faith that does not waver between weakness and strength, depression and assurance, self-pity and courage.

When some heavy physical labor has to be done, do not depend on yourself alone to do it. Do not strain every muscle and sinew to perform the task. You do not have to. God is your strength. Acknowledge His indwelling presence. Let Him work through you to meet the demand. You can work easily, successfully; without straining or injuring your body. You can become strong in the Lord, just as Abraham did. Speak to the wall and muscles of your abdomen, saying:

*You are strong in the strength of the Lord, built up by His enduring substance, repaired and made new by His power.*

Let God help you bear the load. Let Him help you do the lifting. Bear constantly in mind the thought *"God is my strength, unfailing, quick."*

# The Great Repair Shop

THE SPLEEN has been one of the most maligned organs of the body, probably because it has been one of the least understood.

To know any part of the body is much like knowing a person. If you really know and understand a person you invariably find much to love in him. Likewise with the body. When we begin to know and understand it as the living temple that God, our Creator, has provided for us, we come to love and appreciate every cell, organ, and function. The body is as quick to respond to appreciation as is a person.

We used to think of the spleen as the seat of various emotions or passions, to associate it with anger, ill humor, and the like. Disagreeable people were spoken of as splenetics, and the organ was thought of as if it were a sort of inner dumping ground for all that was undesirable.

Now we are beginning to recognize the spleen as the great repair shop of the body. We have discovered that it helps to form red blood cells, life, and substance for us. It also has much to do with the formation of the white blood cells which protect and defend the body.

We hear the spleen spoken of as the great reservoir of life in which are stored numerous red cells. When hemorrhage or loss of energy through heavy exercise or excessive work takes place, the spleen sends forth its reserves to renew and restore us to strength.

Some physiologists claim that the spleen takes part in the production of immunizing substances that develop a resistance to infection within us. Whatever its action along this line, we know that it is our friend, a defender, protector, and repair agent.

Let us then no longer associate untoward emotions, moods, or passions with the spleen. You know how grateful you feel toward the workman who comes and remodels your home, how happy you are with the redecorated walls, refinished floors, gleaming woodwork, and weather-proof roof and cellar. We seek the aid of repair men for almost everything we possess, from shoes to automobiles and houses. We would never dream of blaming the one who does our repair work for us for the conditions demanding attention. Rather we would accept his counsel and co-operate with him in his work.

Think of your spleen henceforth as your very good friend that works faithfully with you to keep your body in perfect repair. It never deserts you in time of emergency, but should such an occasion arise it would instantly send forth its upbuilding substances. Never blame your spleen for vexatious conditions, or excuse morbidity, ill temper, or uncontrolled passions in yourself on the ground that your spleen is out of order. Rather co-operate with this organ by regenerating your thoughts and desires, under the guidance of the Holy Spirit. Be willing to let God remodel your life if need be, to put your thoughts, body, and affairs in perfect order and repair.

God's work in the midst of you is redemptive and restorative. If you feel that your good has been wrested from you or that others should make amends to you, just forget your personal grievance for the time being. Turn about and see what you can do within your own heart and mind to retrieve your good, your joy, your faith, your peace. You have a great reserve of good thoughts within you. Use them now to repair the broken places, to build up harmony and good will, to re-establish your life on a better basis.

Be willing to work toward your perfect regeneration in Christ Jesus, to build your life and consciousness on the foundation of purity, love, harmony, and good cheer. Thank God for the divine law of reparation that makes it possible for every error to be righted, every shortcoming to be corrected, every seeming break in life to be repaired. Praise Him for the restoration taking place in your body as you boldly and fearlessly affirm:

*Father, I thank Thee for a perfect spleen. I thank Thee for the provision of an organ within my body that helps to make me immune to disease while it ceaselessly and harmoniously carries on its priceless service of rebuilding the blood cells that mean life to my body. Bless my mind with divine understanding. Let my every desire be subject to Thy holy desire for me. Let every emotion, impulse, motive, and thought glorify Thee. Let Thy will be done in me and in all my affairs. Father, I thank Thee that Thou hast heard me and that I am now being lifted up and regenerated through the perfect Christ life.*

Yield yourself completely to God's restorative, regenerative power. He will repair your body, renew your mind, adjust your affairs.

# Truth Sweetens and Restores

SUGAR IS a source of warmth and energy for the body. It is essential to the well-being of the physical man that the sugar content of his body should be kept well balanced. Likewise it is essential to the growth of the spiritual man that the sweetness and grace of the Christ character should permeate the personal man and give grace and harmony to every thought, word, and activity.

The pancreas, a gland shaped somewhat like a hammer, lies back of the stomach, quite close to both liver and spleen. Two secretions are formed in the pancreas. The pancreatic fluid, one of the most important digestants, is spoken of as an external secretion. It is valuable to the intestinal digestion. The internal secretion, from which insulin has been extracted, is absorbed by the blood and carried to the tissues. It aids in the oxidation of glucose and the control and use of the sugar content of the body.

Closely associated with the pancreas are the adrenal glands functioning in connection with the kidneys, the pituitary gland at the base of the brain, and the other endocrine glands. The combined work of these glands reveals something of the wonderfully intelligent manner in which the equilibrium of the body is maintained, the secretions and excre-

## Truth Sweetens and Restores

tions guarded and regulated, and the perfect metabolism, renewal, and upbuilding processes carried on.

When we come truly to know and appreciate the body, we find that in its interwoven functioning it points us to the Christ, the superman, the Son of God; for in the balanced and perfectly co-ordinated work of the body we find outpictured the closely interwoven and perfectly co-ordinated work of the Christ Mind in humanity as well as in the individual.

The pancreas, sometimes called the stomach sweetbread, not only aids digestion and regulates the sugar content of the body but also helps to counteract acidity. It points us to the truth that when acid conditions arise in the body, the sweetening, harmonizing, influence of the Christ Spirit should be appealed to, accepted, and used.

In physical disturbances such as diabetes, it is well to hold fast to the all-powerful healing grace of Christ, who abides in you. He will give expression to the healing, harmonizing, restorative life of God in and through you. In every possible way let the love and sweetness of the Christ be made manifest through you.

There is a limitless energizing power in the love of God that keeps the torch of faith burning high in the soul. It quickens every cell in the body with the warm glow of divine life. It strengthens every organ in its functioning and converts every organic activity into a mighty stream of harmonizing life.

I know by experience that children instantly respond to the thought of God as love. God is love. Little children are close to the kingdom of God. They are of His kingdom, the realm of divine love.

When a child's body apparently is not functioning properly, let the adult who cares for it open his heart and mind to the unfailing love of God. Let the mother or the nurse realize that God's love sounds through her voice as she speaks to her child, God's love flows from her finger tips as she cares for it, God's love fills her with understanding, patience, and joy. God's love heals. It rounds out the child's mind and body. It builds up and completely restores. Let the child pray:

*God loves and heals me now. I am His child. I am happy, free, well, and strong.*

The adult is removed from childhood by only a few short years, which are man's measuring rods of time and not God's. Man is equally close to God's kingdom of love, wholeness, harmony. It is within him and about him, for God's kingdom is God's omnipresence.

• Have you ever thought of God as a harsh, unyielding power, a presence holding a vengeful hammer ready to wield in judgment upon you or someone else? If you have, put all such thoughts definitely out of your mind. If you have had any tendency to find fault with others, let such inclinations be put away forever. Remember the work of that

## Truth Sweetens and Restores

hammer-shaped gland lying behind your stomach as it sends its sweetening influence through your body.

For the blessing of your pancreas, turn to Christ, the perfect builder within you. Let your body, your disposition, your desires, your whole self be lifted up to Him as you affirm:

*My life is ordered, sweetened, adjusted, and built up by the power of the indwelling Christ. Every bitter, sour, condemning thought is forgiven and washed away. Every feeble, weak idea has been replaced by one of divine strength and constructive power. I bless my pancreas and co-operate with it in its good work by sending it my Christ-inspired thoughts of divine order and wholeness.*

Look up to Jesus Christ and be healed. Your physical inharmony has served its purpose. It has directed you to Him. You now behold the perfection of the Christ body, and you are bringing it forth.

# *Restoration of Kidneys*

TRUTH CARRIES you beyond the adage "Where there is life there is hope" into the perfect realization that where God is there is certainty. You can be sure of God, sure of His healing love, sure that His power will work for you.

Frequently the question is anxiously asked "Can Bright's disease, diabetes, and dropsy be healed?" Certainly they can, and in no healing is a greater redemptive work of both mind and body accomplished. When the aid of the Great Physician is sought for the healing of physical conditions that affect the regulation of the sugar, water, or albumin content of the body, thus involving the kidneys, the first result noticed is a decided uplift of thought. The mental and emotional reactions to circumstances and conditions are immediately improved. It is as though the light of Jesus Christ touched the mind, freed it from all misgiving, ignorance, darkness, fear, and confusion, and re-established it in confidence, hope, and cheer.

The forgiving love of Jesus Christ comes into the heart and eliminates misunderstanding and bitterness. His pure Spirit redeems the whole man, and thoughts and feelings are cleansed and lifted up into the light of God's perfect, healing love.

## Restoration of Kidneys

There are times when adults and also little children are almost starved for a bit of appreciation and praise. They long for the sweet tenderness of understanding and love. They overindulge in outer sweets and surfeit the system with sugar. Again, there may be a demand of the appetite for animal food or stimulants that must be overcome. Who is so capable of righting and satisfying these unbalanced desires as the Christ? Who can so quickly and surely eliminate the toxins and impurities and renew and reestablish both mind and body in divine order and harmony?

The work of redeeming and healing the body is a glad and joyous one. Pain is but the call to come up higher where we may realize that we are all members of the universal Christ body and as such have a definite place, an active part in Him.

When one member of your body is healed your whole body rejoices. Likewise when you are restored to health the Christ body is given more complete expression and His healing consciousness finds an outlet through you. Love, joy, and faith, flowing freely through your mind, restore you and help to cleanse the race consciousness of inharmony and disease. Do not fear disease. Rather turn infirmity into opportunity and be lifted up into the wholeness of Christ.

Let down the barriers of personal need or desire, yes, even the need of personal healing, as you repeat or sing, "Fill me now to overflowing with thy Holy Spirit, Lord." Be still and know that the ever-increasing tide of God's forgiving love is flowing through you. It is washing away old fears, bitterness, doubts, misunderstanding, and anxiety. Willingly, gladly let them go. It is cleansing your body, freeing it from toxins or impurities as it blesses, refreshes, and restores every organ and cell.

"Fill me now to overflowing with thy Holy Spirit, Lord." God is answering your call. You are filled with the spirit of divine wholeness. Its overflowing measure of joy, assurance, life, and freedom is restoring you. You are passing on to others the healing love of God.

*"The joy of the Lord is your strength."* You are strong in Him, strong enough to lay hold of Truth, wise enough to let go of every thought or condition that could in any way retard your perfect healing. The strong current of divine life flows freely through you. Your mind as well as your kidneys is blessed with perfect elimination.

The source of all life is within you. The wisdom of Divine Mind is within you. The wholeness, peace, purity, and harmony of the Holy Spirit are within you. Your confidence is restored. You are quickened, cleansed, vitalized, and healed. Praise God!

# *Divinely Directed*

DIVINE order rules the body. Consider the orderly, clean, systematic way in which the bladder functions.

Before I heard of Unity or had thought about metaphysics I cared for a patient suffering from cystitis. She was so unhappy, nervous, and irritable that I became interested in helping her overcome her mental condition. She was a very religious person, but her religion seemed only to increase her morbid tendencies.

One day I said to her, "Come, let us play a game together. We both believe that the Spirit of Jesus Christ can cleanse our life. Let us both cast off something that has no further purpose in our life; let us make up our minds to give up some irritable, unhappy thought habit. There is nothing to be gained by holding onto things or thoughts that should be cast off. Each day let us talk things over and see who advances fastest toward the goal of Christian peace and amiability."

The woman almost shrieked at me, "Cast off things! Do you know that is all my life has been, a dumping ground for cast-off things! Even though we had abundance when I was a child, my thrifty parents thought I should finish wearing out my sister's outgrown clothing. Even the house I live in is one unwanted by the rest of the family. All I have ever had was cast-off crusts! You and your high and mighty ideas!"

Gently, patiently I tried to work with the woman. Gradually she began to accept the light. We talked about the trouble she had been having with her bladder, and how when functioning normally it harmoniously disposes of fluid containing certain materials no longer needed by the body. We saw the harm of holding onto anything that was no longer needed. Also we discovered, as the action of the bladder showed so clearly, that there is a right way and a right time to dispose of every surplus.

We became thoroughly interested in disposing of the cast-off things her family had given her. With the most kindly intent in the world, a large circle of relatives had seemed bent on deluging the woman with food, clothing, plants, supplies of all kinds that they no longer needed or wanted.

As the woman opened her heart to others and began to direct the surplus toward those who could use it to good advantage, her life changed for the better.

Day by day we schooled ourselves to let some anxious, disturbing, unkind, or unjust thought be washed away as we immersed our thoughts in God's understanding love and wisdom. Logically, as we did this, a clean, sweet current of life flowed through

## Divinely Directed

us and we began to comprehend and appreciate the good service the bladder rendered.

Have you been reading this book? Do you begin to see what it means to appreciate and love and bless your body? If you do, these lessons have served their purpose, for you are learning of the divinely directed power of life that is in you.

Gradually the woman with whom I was working became less irritable, unhappy, and nervous, and I acquired a deeper understanding and patience. We asked Jesus Christ to direct His cleansing stream of life through her. Then came a time when she slept the night through with no irritation, no discomfort, no pain. The bladder that had troubled her for years began to function properly. Acidity disappeared from her system. In a short time she was healed, happier in mind, more comfortable in body than she had been for years.

Your bladder handles cast-off material for which your body has no further use. It retains the fluid excreted by the kidneys until it can be disposed of in an orderly way. Drinking the right amount of fresh, clean water will frequently allay bladder irritation, just as partaking of the water of life, the refreshing instruction of Jesus, will do away with mental irritation. When the two are combined it means an inner as well as outer cleansing and healing.

To bless the bladder say:

*The inflow and outflow of everything in my life is established in divine order and harmony. Every cell in my body is bathed in the living water of life. Wisdom and good judgment attend me in all my ways. Divine order is established. I am peaceful and poised. Every irritating, unworthy, uncomfortable thought, impulse, or sensation is banished from my body. Christ in the midst of me reigns supreme.*

For children who need help, declare:

*Every organ in your body is under divine control. Christ in the midst of you reigns supreme. Habits of cleanliness, comfort, and order are established in your body. You are God's perfect child.*

# *Body Renewal*

HAVE YOU ever watched a building take shape? Have you seen the great steel girders swing into place and breathlessly watched the riveters at work? Have you stood thrilled before the fragrant lumber, the material for a home, your own perhaps, and joyously watched the carpenters erect the framework? Was ever music sweeter than the sound of the hammers that are building a home?

Yet, all architectural plans that make the skyscraper possible, all the dreams and love that go into the making of a home, are comparatively nothing when you think of the divine wisdom that planned the framework of your body, the love that called it forth, the workmanship that became manifest in it, and the ever-renewing life that was built into every supporting or protective bone.

The very life and substance of God permeate your bones. His strength supports them. They give stability to the whole structure of your body, protect and shelter its vital organs, and preserve its shape. Bless them with the realization that they are strong, stable, well molded, and enduring. Should there be any need for bone repair or adjustment, use your Christ-quickened faith to know that the pure life of God now rebuilds, and restores your body.

Speak this word for yourself, speak it for the bone that needs renewing or strengthening or adjusting:

*The pure life and substance of God now renews, rebuilds, and repairs my body. Every bone is rightly adjusted, made strong, and perfect.*

The healing power of Jesus goes forth to the cripple or the handicapped to straighten, strengthen, and make whole. Rickets, brittle, misshapen, and soft bones, and bones that have suffered through injury or disease will every one respond to His life-restoring word.

You need not be afraid of falling or suffering injury to your bones from it. Underneath are the everlasting arms. You are supported by the strength of God. Your feet are securely directed in the way of Truth. Icy paths need hold no dread for you.

The integrity of Spirit keeps you upright and secure. Relax your muscles. Let God direct you. Dispel every tense, fearful thought with the phrase from *The Prayer of Faith* "God walks beside me, guides my way."

Never give way to the thought of brittle bones. It is an old-age idea that must be overcome if you would retain a youthful, well-regulated, harmonious body. Keep your mind filled with substance thoughts. Avoid all thoughts of insufficiency or lack.

I learned by experience the wisdom of keeping my mind free from thoughts of lack. At one time I

## Body Renewal

had a good many obligations to meet and was questioning how they could be met when I stepped off a streetcar in front of an oncoming automobile. I was pinned beneath it, the front wheel resting on my leg just below the knee. Praise God for the knowledge of Truth that came to sustain me then! As I directed those who gathered to lift the car off my leg, I was thinking with all my might: *"My body is pure God substance. It cannot be broken."* I shall never forget the look of amazement on several faces when I stood up and walked to the curb. There were deep bruises, but they served only to remind me of the necessity of keeping allegiance to my faith in the substance of God. I found an accompanying assurance of supply coming to me: *"God's substance is my supply. It cannot be depleted. There is no lack of life or substance anywhere."*

Many healing needs reveal a belief in lack that should be corrected. Your bones, the framework and support of your body, symbolize your substance and stability in Truth. Let all who need a greater certainty of stability and substance in mind, body, or affairs turn to God.

"If thou return to the Almighty, thou shalt be built up."

# *Joyous and Free*

"YE SHALL know the truth, and the truth shall make you free." Now let your body rejoice in the joy and freedom of Jesus Christ. Let every joint become receptive to His healing power. Let every cell glorify Him with perfect health.

Jesus Christ is now with you quickening within you a faith that is sure and unfailing. In His name you can send the word of wholeness to any part of your body temple or speak it to others and call forth the perfect life of Spirit.

Bless your joints with the thought of joy and freedom. Arthritis can be prevented and healed. Rheumatism can be cured. Give thanks for the freedom your joints permit you to enjoy as they enable you to assume different positions, to walk easily, to use your hands, to move your head. A creaking or painful joint can be so lubricated with the oil of joy that it will work perfectly, but you must let go of every unyielding, bigoted, or set thought that acts as a joy-killer and let Christ lead you in the joyous understanding of His gospel of freedom and wholeness.

Joy is a perfect lubricant. It lightens all burdens. It counteracts sorrow and does away with depression. Isaiah tells of the One who gives the "oil of joy for mourning, the garment of praise for the spirit of

## Joyous and Free

heaviness." There is strength and uplift in the joy of the Lord, there is freedom in it. It is a powerful healing agent.

Permit nothing to stand between you and the joy that is yours in Christ. Let go of every thought that causes you unhappiness. It may be a thought of pain or disease, an idea that you are not loved or wanted, a belief in old age, injustice, failure, lack, inharmony, or an unbending pride. Loose such thoughts and let them go. Then let the freeing, uplifting, joy-inspiring thoughts that the Christ inspires come into your mind and heal you.

Be thankful for every outer or inner thing that promotes happiness and freedom. Be glad for every evidence of good that you see in the lives of others. Rejoice in the blessings that come to them. There are equal blessings in store for you.

Whatever tends to make you freer, to increase your consciousness of joy, think on those things. Thousands of things surrounding you reveal the freedom of Spirit that created them. A bird soaring in the blue vault of heaven at eventide, a stream tumbling joyously down a hillside, a rose giving forth its fragrance with every opening petal, a star sending its light across fathomless space.

From within and without there constantly comes to you God's blessing of freedom and joy. Listen each day to the glad song of life within you, the song of life about you. David was not the only one inspired to psalms of joy, but he was the one who gave expression to them. You can be a David too. You can give expression to the joy of Spirit. You can loose the bond and set yourself and others free. Use this healing prayer:

*Father, I thank Thee for perfect freedom. I thank Thee for the "oil of joy" that is now blessing every joint in my body. I partake of the fullness of Thy joy. Every part of my body glorifies Thee in joy and unity. All stiffness, pain, soreness, discomfort, give way to the healing spirit of Thy joy. I am unbound, straight, free, happy, and well. I am healed, praise God, I am healed.*

"Ye shall go out with joy, and be led forth with peace: the mountains and the hills shall break forth before you into singing."

# *Responsibility*

THE SHOULDERS represent responsibility. Perhaps in no other phase of life's expression does Truth help more definitely to set man free than through the enlightenment it affords concerning responsibilities.

We all know how happily and usefully, a little child develops as it is permitted to share certain home responsibilities, how its intelligence is brought into action, how its interest in the home is increased. Home duties, lovingly and wisely assigned by the parents and willingly, consciously shared by the child, make him realize his important part and place in the family group. It builds him up in self-respect and consideration for others. As he becomes responsible he gains confidence and proves himself capable and trustworthy. The child has taken his initial step toward independence and success, and he is justly proud of it. He is happier, more content, and better off in every way. So it is with the adult who willingly performs his allotment of service in establishing God's kingdom here on earth. He takes his right place as a citizen of that kingdom and enjoys all its benefits. He helps to carry on the greater works of the Son of God.

Responsibilities are a stimulant to growth. When

shared with God they are the power that clears the way for higher, ever higher development and achievement. On the other hand, when responsibility is grudgingly accepted, unwillingly borne, and complemented with self-pity and a sense of martyrdom, it is soon magnified into a burden that weighs down and warps mind, body, and soul.

"Come unto me, all ye that labor and are heavy laden, and I will give you rest. Take my yoke upon you, and learn of me; for I am meek and lowly in heart: and ye shall find rest unto your souls. For my yoke is easy, and my burden is light."

The yoke of Jesus Christ will diminish the weight of your burdens. It will make your shoulders light and free. Working with Him, yoked together with Him in spirit, your every responsibility will be discharged with ease and in order, and you will daily grow toward the stature of the Christ man who can do all things.

Remember that responsibilities are soul expanders when rightly assumed and willingly, wisely, lovingly borne. God has gauged your inner strength. He knows your divine possibilities. In the name of the Son, He has given you a helper that will go with you every step of the way.

Bless your shoulders with this thought and watch them grow strong and straight:

*God is blessing me now with courage, strength, and understanding. I no longer bear the load alone.*

*I no longer regret my responsibilities. I have accepted the yoke of Jesus Christ. He shares my burdens. Henceforth I live, work, and rest in His mighty love and power. My shoulders are blessed by the lightness of His yoke. They are braced and strengthened by the power of His comprehending love. Upright and free, I join my fellow men to bless them every one in the name of the Christ that lives and works through me.*

# Encircling Love

IT WAS THE arms of Jesus extended upon the cross that revealed to the world the all-encompassing love of God. It was the arms of Jesus infolding little children as He blessed them that revealed the incomparable mothering love of our Father-Mother God.

The shoulder joint in which the arms are joined to the body, is the most freely movable joint in the body. It betokens your free use of the love of God. You have it within you to encircle all things with love, and love never fails in its divine overcoming.

How different the arms of God, the power of divine love and intelligence that encircles humanity with loving-kindness, from the arms of men, when they are lifted up in strife or greedily reaching out for material possessions. How different the arms of Jesus, extended in good will and peace, from the destructive arms of war, the forces of greed, hatred, suspicion, and fear.

The arms and hands are the "doers of the word," the executors of the Golden Rule. Your arms may be extended from your shoulders to scatter blessings of life, love, and substance, or they may form a circle that will forever remind you of the all-encompassing love of God. Bless your arms with the realiza-

*Encircling Love*

tion of spiritual action and power. You can infold anyone who is suffering from sickness, anyone who needs solace or comfort, anyone whom God directs to you—you can encircle one and all, even those whom you may have termed enemies—with the divine love that has quickened your soul.

You can lift up your arms in praise and thanksgiving to God. You can reach down and give some fellow creature a lift. The arm of God is not so shortened that it cannot save, neither need your arms be hampered, crippled, swollen, or impaired so that they cannot do the blessed work of the Father.

Bless your arms. Praise them, saying:

*I give thanks to God for perfect arms. I bless Him that it is now possible for me to extend His gifts to the world. I am thankful that I can encircle all people, all things with love, even as Christ has done. Bless God for my arms. Bless Him for His love that has made them strong, free, symmetrical, and perfect.*

# Your Helpful Hands

THE HANDS have been likened to the executive power of the mind because through the hands the decree of the will is put into execution. Your mind is blessed with the power to think and to will; your heart is endowed with the power to feel and to love; your hands are equipped to carry into effect the thoughts you think and the things you feel.

No part of the body displays a greater intelligence than the hands or teaches a more perfect lesson in obedience. Without a second's hesitation your hands carry out the orders of your mind. When mind, heart, and hands work in unison, a mighty volume of love, tenderness, substance, and intelligence is put into the work at hand.

Think of the hands of a mother as she cares for her home, a father as he works day by day to provide for his family, a nurse as she tends her patient. What a world of comfort and assurance can pass through those hands!

Think of the gift-filled hands of Jesus as He went about among the people healing, uplifting, feeding, and blessing them. Think of your own hands. Look at them. Have you ever truly appreciated them and the ceaseless service they render?

Love, the divine executor, finds a wonderful out-

## Your Helpful Hands

let through your hands, as does every other divine quality.

Meditate on the affirmation: *God is my perfect will; through me it is done.* Let the thought linger in your mind until its full meaning comes to you.

The hands are the obedient servants of the will. When you realize that it is through you that God's perfect will is done in the world, when you surrender all personal willfulness and are ready to do His will, when you yield every turbulent, anxious, resistant thought to the certainty that His will is always good, then and not until then will you fully appreciate your hands and the holy office they are equipped to fulfill.

Can your life be separated from the life of God? Is your mind a thinking apparatus independent of Divine Mind? Can your heart be isolated from the infinite heart of divine love? No; nor are your hands distinct from the hand of God.

Your hands are God's hands, ready and capable of performing perfect service. Bless them and let them carry out His excellent plans. Love them and let them work for God, for humanity, for your family, for you. Do not drive them, force them, abuse them, or think of them as gnarled, crooked, hard, rough, or unlovely. Praise your hands, appreciate them, thank God for perfect hands.

Your hand bears the imprint of your character, your individuality. It also bears the imprint of your heart, life, and mind. It represents the acme of faith that can lay hold of all good, the essence of love that can dispense all good, the purpose of life that has its foundation in the law of giving and receiving. Your hand is fashioned to carry out in the world about you the creative law of divine order, harmony, and beauty.

No matter what your work may be, as you perform it know that the life, love, and peace of God is flowing through your hands. Consider the intelligence of each finger tip. It is relaying the will of God into your work.

*God is my perfect will; through me it is done. My hands are God's hands. They bear His gift of life, love, and beauty. They execute His will in the world of affairs. My fingers are straight and perfect. Life streams from every tip, a healing current to the world. My hands are strong and gracious in God's service. Smooth and gentle they are, for I have put condemnation, irritation, cruelty, rough things, hard things, out of my life forever.*

The function of your hands, God's hands, is to bring heaven to earth and to lift earth to heaven. God bless your precious hands!

# *Independence*

WHILE THE shoulders represent responsibility, the hips represent individual independence, free will, and self-support. They perform a most important function in locomotion and make it possible for a person to move his body about, to follow new pathways.

The shoulders, which help to form the walls of the chest cavity that contains the heart and lungs, which are so closely akin to the spiritual nature of life, are counterbalanced by the hips. The hipbones help to form the pelvic basin that supports the generative organs. These are closely associated with the formation of the personal, physical life.

The hipbone also contains the socket into which the head of the femur or thighbone fits. This joint makes it possible for man to sit down and to move around. How often we hear persons express the wish that they might sit at the feet of some master and be taught by him. So our hips, the seat of physical life, remind us that we may turn within and in Spirit sit at the feet of Jesus Christ and learn of Him the lessons we need to know. Then we may go out among our fellow men and put His teachings into actual practice in our daily life and affairs.

Avoid feeling that spiritual things are suitable

only for Sabbath-day consideration or emergencies but are too exalted, ethereal, or impractical for adaptation to the common happenings of the everyday life. Do not draw a line between your independence as a human being and your spiritual dependence on God as His offspring.

Rejoice that you may stand on your own feet and direct them in the way of Truth. Rejoice that you are inherently self-supporting. When a person selfishly or needlessly depends too completely on others to support him and arrange his affairs for him, he cripples his own abilities.

At a class meeting Charles Fillmore said, "Never make the mistake of trying to shut God up in your mind, or lock Him in your heart, or put Him on a high pedestal where He may be inaccessible to you in your momently need. Bring your realization of God right down into your own body; bring His executive power right out into your affairs. Find God in every walk of life. Then shall you abide in Omnipresence. Then shall you know liberty and freedom."

As you go about in the business world, the world of service, or your own home world, take God with you. If problems arise that puzzle, annoy, or frighten you, turn within. Keep your mind calm and receptive as you sit down in the silence before your inner Lord and Teacher and let Him instruct you in the way of order, peace, and Christian co-operation. Let the blessed assurance of your spiritual realization be

# Independence

made manifest in your physical life and world as you use this affirmation:

*I am free and whole in the omnipresence of God. I sit under the counsel of the Almighty. I walk among my fellow men, independent, self-supporting, and unafraid, conveying the blessings of Truth to them in all that I think, say, and do. Truth is reshaping my life and my body in divine order and perfection. My hips, my legs, are blessed with the pure, free-flowing, formative life and substance of God. I give thanks for their perfection.*

# Devotion and Humility

THE KNEES represent devotion and humility. Kneeling is an act of faith, a bowing of the ego before God. As you grow in Truth you learn how every outer act has its spiritual counterpart. Then you may not kneel on your knees to pray, but you will constantly experience that gracious humility of spirit which so readily yields all things to the Father. The prayer of your innermost heart will be "Let thy will be done." You will know the exaltation of spirit that comes as you realize that your Father's benediction rests constantly upon you.

Like the knight of old who by his knighthood was bound to chivalrous conduct, the personal ego kneels before God, is freed from past weakness or error, and bound by God's redeeming love and wisdom to Christlike conduct.

Sometimes it brings the greatest sense of relief and peace to drop on one's knees to pray, but those priceless moments of communion with the Father should not be limited by the thought that one can pray only when kneeling. It is not the position of the body so much as it is the attitude of mind and heart that expresses true devotion.

So let your knees be to you symbols of devotion, love, grace, and humility rather than agents of some

## Devotion and Humility

religious custom that may bind you to old thoughts and habits that you are perhaps spiritually outgrowing. Let your knees remind you of God's devotion to you, the eternal spirit of loving-kindness that makes itself known through the Scriptures in these words: "I have loved thee with an everlasting love: therefore with loving-kindness have I drawn thee."

Thank God for your blessed knees as you declare:

*God has loved me with an everlasting love. With loving-kindness He has drawn me into the presence of His Holy Spirit. My consciousness is cleansed from all criticism, antagonism, or ill will. God's devotion to me, my devotion to Him, is from everlasting to everlasting. My knees are strengthened and renewed by the power of divine love. They are agile, painless, free.*

# Two Blessed Feet

TWO BLESSED feet! What a treasure they are, what a pleasure to walk on, what a joy to own! You can have them. You can know the joy of perfect freedom. You can enjoy the comfort of perfect feet.

Bless your feet with the single word *Peace*. Bless the paths your feet follow with the thought of peace. Bless your home, your neighborhood, your occupation with the knowledge of peace.

What an intricate pattern the paths that the average person treads daily would weave. What a history of human activities is written in the paths the feet of men have shaped.

What a history of divine love is written along the highway that Jesus trod! Like a golden thread of hope and understanding it runs through the world today. There is a legend of Jesus that says that flowers bloomed in the wilderness where His feet had trod. Surely flowers of wholeness, beauty, purity, and faith blossom along the pathway of Truth where He leads you today.

Your feet reveal more of your life, thoughts, and habits than you may think. They are the parts of your body that come most nearly into direct contact with the earth. They help make the routes

*Two Blessed Feet*

along which the course of your life runs.

What sort of a world are you living in? What is your attitude toward your neighbors? How many burdens are you carrying? Take an inventory of them and see if their weight may not be lessened by trusting entirely in God.

Look to the life path you are mapping, the one you now travel, and see if you have let discontent, misunderstanding, or distrust spring up about you. It is possible for you to traverse the smoothest highway man can build and yet suffer all the discomfort of a cobblestone road if your mind is besieged by cobblestone thoughts.

"How beautiful upon the mountains are the feet of him that bringeth good tidings, that publisheth peace, that bringeth good tidings of good, that publisheth salvation, that saith unto Zion, Thy God reigneth!"

How truly the words of Isaiah applied to the feet of Jesus as they bore Him to and fro on missions of love, joy, kindness, and helpfulness! To the world He brought great tidings of good. He published peace and salvation. He taught the world concerning the inner kingdom where God reigns, the omnipresent kingdom where good is supreme.

The blessed feet of the Saviour have marked a path for your feet to follow. When walking the path that He trod, your feet too are blessed.

Truth puts wings on your feet. Love softens

every hard spot. Wisdom straightens every crooked place. Faith strengthens, lifts up, and supports weak or broken arches. The cleansing power of the Holy Spirit does away with any infection. Joy banishes any inverted, festering thoughts of self-pity as well as any ingrowing nails.

Divine judgment leads you to choose your shoes wisely, so you need not suffer the discomfort of misfit shoes. It also frees your thoughts from limited, boxed-in ideas that hold you in bondage to wrong concepts of God and of the limitless good He has prepared for you.

*Peace.* Speak the word to your feet as you put on your shoes. Speak it to yourself as you start your daily round of activities.

*Peace.* Send your thought of peace to others as you walk along the street. Send it to the government and the leaders of the nations as you read your daily paper.

When you were a child you were taught to march to a rhythmic repetition of "Left, right, left, right, left, right." Think of yourself today as a child of God and march to a rhythmic thought of "Peace, peace, peace, peace" until your relations with the world become perfectly harmonious and peaceful.

Stand upright and unafraid in the presence of God. The way ahead of you is clear. Your feet are swift and beautiful in His sight. Your understanding of Truth is stable, the sure foundation of your

*Two Blessed Feet*  141

body. Every advancing step you take leaves an imprint of Truth that makes the way easier and more beautiful for someone else.

*Peace.* Let it be your prayer, your motive, your blessing, your assurance. Peace comes from understanding God, and your feet represent and bear out your understanding of God as good in everybody and everything.

*My understanding is permeated and controlled by the all-pervading peace of God. I go swiftly, courageously, joyously forward to the goal of my high calling in Christ Jesus. My mind is clear, my thoughts poised in Truth, my body perfectly balanced and supported. I thank God for perfect feet, a clear path ahead, and His light all the way. I praise Him for perfect peace.*

"In the name of Jesus Christ of Nazareth, walk."

# Strong Wrists and Ankles

Both the ankles and the wrists may be thought of as important connecting links in the body. While the wrists complete the union of the shoulders, symbols of responsibility, and the arms, which are emblematic of God's all-encircling love, with the hands, the "doers of the word"; the ankles reveal the union of the hips indicative of self-support and independence and the knees, representative of devotion and humility, with the feet, which denote understanding.

Learn to relax your wrists and you will add greatly to the control and efficiency of your hands. Music teachers instruct their pupils to relax the wrists by letting the arms hang loosely from the shoulder and then shaking the wrists limply, like a rag. It is surprising how all the tenseness and the aching pain will leave the arms and fingers, and how much more readily and intelligently the hands will execute the work in hand. Every finger will tingle with new life, every one will react with greater agility and responsiveness.

Your wrists can teach you a valuable lesson in relaxation. They can prove to you how rapidly your inherent ability can flow through your arms and hands. They are links, but there is nothing forced

## Strong Wrists and Ankles

or rigid about them. You do not have to stiffen them. By relaxation their strength is increased. If you have to carry water or use your hands and arms for heavy lifting, let your wrists relax as you declare:

*I thank God for the perfect union between my desire to do and my ability to accomplish. I praise Him for strong, supple, perfect wrists.*

It is the steady pull that moves the load. You do not have to jerk or strain or overexert yourself in order to accomplish your tasks. Relax your shoulders, arms, and wrists. At the same time rejoice in your perfect union with God, a union that brings you into the freedom and grace, the limitless strength and ability of His Holy Spirit.

Even as your wrists increase the efficiency of your hands, so your ankles increase the freedom of your feet. They make your step agile and secure. They help to balance your body and to keep it upright. They add grace and freedom to your walk.

Daily praise God for your perfect ankles. Do you recall how the man by the gate of the Temple called Beautiful leapt up rejoicing when Peter said to him, "In the name of Jesus Christ of Nazareth, walk." The man sought alms because he considered himself a hopeless cripple. Instead of the coin the beggar sought Peter extended to him the greater gift, even the faith that heals. How thankful, how radiantly happy the man must have been.

Ankle chains with balls attached, old-time ankle

stocks are symbolic of the bondage of man before he becomes aware of his spiritual understanding. If you have any trouble with your ankles, be still before the Christ who abides in you and acknowledge your perfect union with His understanding light and love. Let Him reveal the Christ way to you, the way of divine understanding, the path made safe by the knowledge of Truth. Let Him quicken your life, your heart, your consciousness with His God-revealing gospel of good will and peace. Bless your ankles in His name, saying:

*In the name of Jesus Christ and by His power you are quickened, strengthened, and healed.*

As you daily keep up the work of spiritually redeeming your body from every form of disease or error you will be obeying the admonition of Paul, who said, "I beseech you therefore, brethren, by the mercies of God, to present your bodies a living sacrifice, holy, acceptable to God, *which is* your spiritual service. And be not fashioned according to this world: but be ye transformed by the renewing of your mind, that ye may prove what is the good and acceptable and perfect will of God."

# Perfect Co-ordination

WE HEAR and read much about the importance of co-operation. It is the keynote of harmonious living, therefore it is well that we should give it our attention. However we need not go outside our own body temple to find working and in order the most nearly perfect co-operative system known to man.

Nerves, muscles, and the bones that make up the framework of the body are so closely co-ordinated that the degree of usefulness of any one of them depends on the development and proper functioning of the others.

Consider the muscular system. An armor of strength and power, responsive, intelligent, and protective, the muscles carry on one of the most important functions of the body. They make possible various movements, many of which, such as breathing and the beating of the heart, we never consider, so accustomed are we to their perfect activity.

Muscles may be likened to mighty dynamos that are capable of converting chemical energy into mechanical energy. Perhaps no organ of the body reveals a greater sense of power, surely none is more obedient to the command of the mind.

In time of emergency muscles have risen to the

occasion and accomplished almost unbelievable feats of strength. If you have walked through a dark room, even though you were moving slowly and carefully, and brought your toe in contact with the rocker of a chair or some other solid object, you know something of the energy expended in so simple a thing as walking. Yet were it not for the commands sent along the nerves by the brain and the prompt, unquestioning obedience of the muscles to those commands, the muscles would be of no use to us. They would only bring about confusion, disorder, and helplessness.

Are muscles seemingly weak, unresponsive, paralyzed? Go direct to Jesus Christ, the inner source of divine power. He who healed the man with the withered hand, commanding him, "Stretch forth thy hand," will likewise heal you.

In the name of Jesus Christ you can declare the word of energy, strength, power. Fill your mind with positive, energizing thoughts. Center your faith in the vitalizing power of the Holy Spirit. Then co-operate with your faith and know that every nerve carries a message of life and energy to the muscle that needs quickening. Declare:

*In the name of Jesus Christ I send the message of life along every nerve in my body. My muscles now co-operate with the perfect Christ idea of life. I am obedient and responsive to the divine law of life. Every muscle in my body is quickened, vitalized, strengthened, and restored.*

## Perfect Co-ordination

Are muscles contracted, painful, cramped? Open your mind and heart to God. Rest in the assurance that His love is infolding you, His wisdom is mapping your way. Let mind and body relax as you affirm:

*I now let go of every thought of willfulness, limitation, futility. I release all my affairs into God's keeping. I do not seek to have my own way. I am willing to let God's will be done in and through me. Love of God, I rest in you. Peace of God, I welcome you. Life of God, I cherish you. I give thanks for perfect co-ordination in my mind, body, and affairs.*

Muscles, like faith, are strengthened as they are rightly used. They are your talisman of power, vitality, energy, and grace. You are strong, you are unbound, you are harmonious in mind and in body. Thank God.

# *Healing Blessing*

PEACE BE unto you, peace and poise in mind and in body. Now may the harmonizing blessing of Jesus Christ be conveyed along every nerve. Now may His assurance of life, love, and abundance free you from fear, anxiety, and worry.

In order to serve you properly your nervous system has to be and is quickly responsive, highly sensitive to every command of your mind. Because they are so responsive to thought the nerves react immediately to Truth. Instantaneous relief from nervous disorders can be gained at once by centering your thoughts in a single harmonizing word.

For instance, take such words as *peace, love, life, courage, joy,* and the like, and let your thoughts branch out from the word that is most applicable to your need. It will attract other words and phrases and build up inspired thoughts of Truth, such as:

"God is peace. His peace now soothes and relaxes all tension or distress."

"God is love. His love surrounds me. Love fears no enemy, no disease, no evil. I rest in love. It harmonizes my life and blesses me in all my ways."

"God is my rufuge of strength and courage. I am fearless, and courageous. My nerves are steady, strong and dependable."

## Healing Blessing

"God is life. I am not at cross-purposes with anybody or anything. I am poised and centered in the life of God. I send His word of life coursing along every nerve in my body. God's life knows no fatigue, no depletion, no irritation. My every nerve is alert, alive, harmonious; my mind is established in the perfect life of God."

"God has given me the Spirit of joy. Joy now supersedes gloom, depression, and touchiness in my consciousness. Truth makes me free, happy, glad. My nerves react to the spirit of freedom and happiness. They carry the realization of joyous living to every part of my body."

You can bless your nerves through relaxation; also you can build them up by varying your work. Life should never be monotonous, tragic, or undesirable to you. If your days are ruled by routine and your work seems humdrum, your existence dull and drab, you should inject some variety, some happy thoughts into your daily mode of living. God reveals the way to you.

Personally I find that a sturdy, "friendly" walk or a bit of outdoor work, accompanied by kindly, happy, "God-bless-you" thoughts is the best nerve tonic in the world. By a friendly walk I mean one in which I watch for something to smile at, something toward which I can direct a thought of love and helpful blessing. Whether it is a crowded city street where one building follows another in quick succession or a country lane with no habitation in sight there is always something to merit my kindly thought. It may be a little child, a stranger passing by, an animal, or a clump of friendly trees beside a winding, singing brook. Even though I may have but fifteen minutes to spare I find that I can scatter a world of blessings in even so short a time and return to my indoor work refreshed and renewed.

When one completely abandons one's self, enjoying and blessing the things at hand, the Spirit of Christ possesses one, and His light, love, life, and substance quicken and revitalize every nerve.

As you steadily let thoughts of God and Truth occupy your mind and accompany you in all that you do, there will be no question about your night's rest. You grow to know God intimately, to trust Him definitely and completely. Perfect trust in God is the secret of perfect relaxation, rest, and renewal. It is the remedy for sleeplessness as well as many other ills.

"Come unto me . . . and I will give you rest." The Spirit of Christ abiding in you is blessing you now with a deep, inner consciousness of quietness, assurance, rest, and peace. Rest and restoration are now bestowed on you through the understanding love of Jesus Christ.

# The Solar Plexus

THE SOLAR PLEXUS, one of the largest and most important nerve centers in the body, is located behind the stomach. It has been termed the "body brain" by some because it consists of several ganglia and a dense network of nerve fibers that unite them. Here we find gray matter similar to that found in the brain and along the spinal cord.

The keenest intelligence is displayed in the work of the solar plexus. One definition given for solar is "pertaining to the sun"; the solar system being composed of the sun and the celestial bodies revolving round it. When physiologists gave the name solar plexus to the powerful network of nerves guarding, protecting, and helping control the vital organs, they must have felt that it was a center of light and intelligence round which many vital functions revolved.

The solar plexus reacts instantly to the emotions. It might be termed a buffer and harmonizer for many bodily sensations. Every ecstasy, every pleasure, as well as every sense of tragedy and sorrow registers there. As far as it can it shields the body from excessive sensations. Through divine love and light, ever active in you, you can bring your emotions and sensations under complete control. It is the work of your solar plexus, your illumined nerve center, to relay to your body in an orderly manner, the nerve impulses that you permit and encourage.

We all know how quickly hate, passion, fear, shock, and kindred emotions strike in at the pit of the stomach. We all know that they affect the action of the vital organs, but perhaps some of us have not realized how surely love, purity, courage, poise, and the like enable us to offset and master every adverse, impure, or destructive emotion or desire.

Some teachers align the solar plexus with the soul and the subconsciousness. Some students fear the subconscious mind. To them it is a realm of past error thought, emotions, and karmic existence, a sort of inner hell.

Do you fear your subconscious mind? Do you think your emotions, your nerves, are beyond your control? The light of Christ penetrates your subconscious mind, your soul consciousness, your body consciousness. His intelligence is available to you. His redeeming love adjusts every error. His wisdom establishes you in divine order. You may well liken your subconscious mind to the recording angel of your soul. In it the memory of your blessed association with God from the beginning is kept alive. Through it His grace acts to protect you from destruction, to free you from past error or limitation.

Bless your solar plexus with thoughts such as these:

## The Solar Plexus

*I rejoice in the light of the Son of God, now radiating from the center to the circumference of my being. His pure Spirit cleanses me. His intelligence directs every thought, emotion, and reaction. His love sheds its redeeming glory in my soul. My solar plexus is responsive to love, light, and order. Through it peace, order, and harmony are established in me.*

Now take your Bible and read the 13th chapter of First Corinthians. Place your bookmark at this greatest of all love chapters. Tomorrow read the chapter again, and every day thereafter reread it until you feel the tide of divine love reordering your life in perfect harmony, poise, and bliss.

"And I, if I be lifted up from the earth, will draw all men unto myself."

As you master your emotions, your feelings, your thoughts and desires; as you redeem them under the guidance of Jesus Christ and pattern your activities after the greater works that He has promised that His followers shall do, you will rise out of the entanglements of the mortal man. You will ascend into the consciousness of Christ, the Son of God. You will take on His nature and grow to His stature. Then your life will shine as a sun, warming and cheering the lives of others around you.

# The Silence

THE SILENCE is not foreign to you, a thing you have to reach out after to get. You have it within and about you. You always have had it and you always will have it. It is a part of your eternal nature, a part of God's plan of rest, growth, recuperation, and renewal.

The silence is the holy peace of God active at the heart of all creation. It is the holy peace of God infolding you in the quietness and the security of His presence.

Sacrosanct, all powerful, all glorious the word of God is breathed forth from the heart of the silence. It works through the universal realm. It works through nature's realm. Day after day it sheds the glory of its light upon the earth; night after night brings quiet resting hours to mankind; season after season provides periods of rest and growth to all creation. Silently the seed breaks the clod of earth in which it is imbedded. Silently the green shoot appears, and later the blossom crowns it in beauty. Within every existing thing there is a place of stillness, a depth of quiet. Every cell in your body bears the imprint of God's silent work. Everyone worships Him in silence and wholeness: just by living he worships and honors Him.

## The Silence

Jesus, the man who loved and healed the multitudes, knew the friendly, recuperative power to be found in the quietness of wilderness or mountain fastness. He appreciated the power of the silence that worked through rock and stream, earth and forest. He, who loved God as perhaps no other man has ever done, who loved humanity with a divine selflessness and devotion, learned of an "inner chamber," a place of retreat within the consciousness of each individual. He knew that every man had access to this place of silence, this strong tower of Jehovah.

The inner chamber is the power station of God within you. It is the divine center of consciousness in the midst of your being. When you enter there you lay hold of the power of God. Automatically the door of your thought world closes against doubt, fear, uncertainty, hatred or any other error that might contradict your perfection and wholeness in Christ.

Every cell in your body follows the trend of your thought. When your mind stands at attention before God, when your thoughts are quiet and receptive to Him, every cell receives the benediction of His peace and wholeness. Every one functions in harmony with His Spirit of love, life, and substance. Every one becomes a power station to generate radiant life and health. The peace of Jesus Christ, the peace that He has bestowed upon you, floods your consciousness, your body, your environment.

*Silence.* What a beautiful word it is. How potent with faith! How filled with spiritual radiance. How the light of God's peace illumines it. How its tranquillity rests mind and body.

*Silence.* It is the "pearl of great price," the spiritual balancer of all that is. At night you are blessed by it as you sleep. In the busy hours you are blessed by it as your work. Have you not known this? Have you thought the silence was beyond your experience or comprehension? Watch your hands as they deftly perform their tasks. How silently your fingers move. How quietly your hands serve you. Think of the various functions of your body and the silence maintained by them.

*Silence.* It is as natural to you as is the beating of your heart and equally essential. In the hurry and scurry of personal activities you may have thought that you were withdrawn from it, but that was only your misunderstanding of God's method of expressing Himself through you. Bless God now for the silent power of His Spirit, for the holy retreat within your consciousness, yes, within every cell of your body temple, where you may abide in security, serenity, and perfect poise.

Train yourself to recognize the silence ever existing within and around you. It will establish you in peace of mind, service, and atmosphere. Give yourself an opportunity to stop all activity sometime during each twenty-four hours, and let every bit of

*The Silence*

you—affections, emotions, desires of mind, body, and soul—rest in silent receptivity before God.

The good you seek is seeking you. Clothed in the silence of your divinity, it awaits expression in your life and affairs.

"My soul, wait thou in silence for God only;
 For my expectation is from him.
 He only is my rock and my salvation:
 *He is* my high tower; I shall not be moved.
 With God is my salvation and my glory:
 The rock of my strength, and my refuge, is in God."

*"My soul, wait thou in silence for God only;
 For my expectation is from him."*

# The Generative Organs

THE GENERATIVE organs are the center of reproductive life. No function is capable of fulfilling a more noble purpose from a physical standpoint, and none can carry a person into greater degradation. Through them the heights and the depths of human experience may be known.

The generative organs reveal the faith of God placed in men and women when He intrusted them with the function of reclothing souls entering the world through the birth of children. Likewise they reveal the love that God bestowed upon them, even the parental love of the mother and father.

The reactions of uterus, ovaries, and mammary glands to the pituitary gland, situated at the base of the brain, shows the close relationship of the generative system to the brain, the organ of the mind. It provides a definite and decisive reason why the organs of generation should be carefully guarded against any misuse. Neither should they be made the butt of uncouth jokes or untrue, fantastic tales that so often result in unfortunate conditions in the life of people, especially young people during or immediately following the adolescent period.

Just as one thinks of the heart as the center of love, so one should think of the generative organs

## The Generative Organs

as the center of purity. In his book *The Twelve Powers of Man* Mr. Fillmore speaks of them as the "life center." When they are lowered to animal levels they are Judas, the betrayer of the Christ, the divine self. When their substance is wasted and their divine purpose defiled they become the vortex of base and destructive experiences.

On the other hand, through the birth of little children the generative organs produce the greatest blessing known on the physical plane. This remains true although there are those who have "made themselves eunuchs for the kingdom of heaven's sake." These are they who have chosen to follow Christ Jesus in the regeneration of their lives. They give their substance to the upbuilding of the pure spiritual consciousness, the lifting of the race to the substance of the universal Christ body.

These organs should be understood, held sacred, and consecrated to the perfect will and life of Spirit. Sacredness should take the place of secrecy in all matters pertaining to them.

The time is rapidly passing when any girl will enter puberty uninstructed, unprepared to care for herself intelligently; or any boy will be exposed through ignorance to indulge in practices that are a detriment to him mentally, morally, and physically, as well as a menace to society.

The wise mother teaches her daughter to understand and to respect the generative organs. The wise father instructs his son in the principles of clean, wholesome living. Matters pertaining to the subject of sex are not overemphasized or unduly referred to, neither are they foolishly avoided or misrepresented. Thus the creative organs are protected against childish ignorance and folly. Destructive habits are avoided. Adolescent children are shielded from the effect of unwise and often harmful misleading discussions with others in an endeavor to find out the ways of life.

Be clean minded, frank, and honest with your children. Live purely and teach them to hold sacred and pure the things that pertain to intimate home and family life.

The child who from babyhood has been taught the virtue of clean thoughts, clean hands, a pure heart, constructive recreation and occupation, and self-control is in no danger of becoming involved in sex problems. Help your children to think and carry out creative ideas in their work and in their play. Encourage the spirit of inventiveness that is so rightly a part of childhood. Let them find and follow new ways of doing things so that the natural creative instincts may be constructively and happily used and you will do much to eliminate sexual inquisitiveness and restlessness from their minds.

Remember that the generative organs enshrine the seed of life. When they are lifted up to the Christ plane they act as the chalice bearing the

## The Generative Organs

substance of eternal life to you.

Should there be any need for adjustment for menstrual disorders at the beginning of the period, let your daughter unite with you in this prayer:

*Divine order, purity, and peace are established in me. I welcome my womanhood and consecrate it to Jesus Christ. Poised, happy, healthy, and content, I give thanks to Him.*

As naturally and normally as the menstrual period begins, just so naturally and normally does it cease. There is nothing to fear in the change of life that comes to woman. In fact there is much to look forward to as the body, freed from its reproductive work, is built up in a strong, stable, peaceful structure of life.

If you are approaching or experiencing this change of life and you have any preconceived thoughts of disorder or inharmony associated with it in your mind, let all such thoughts be erased permanently now. Your physical renewal is but the initial step toward the limitless good that awaits you as you fearlessly undergo the good change.

Trusting God for the harmonious adjustment of your body functions, knowing Him as your perfect health, and looking to Him for the inspiration and revealment of the higher and better life that lies ahead, you can suffer no inharmony.

Some things concerning the physical expression of life should always be held sacred. The change of life is one of them. It should not be discussed promiscuously. Women often build up a false fear among themselves by listening to accounts of terrible experiences at this period of life. When traced, these stories are frequently found to be unwarranted, ridiculous tales exaggerated or misrepresented through much repeating.

As easily as one season blends into another, so does one period of life merge into another. The change of life is in reality a time of soul growth and emancipation. Following the good, freeing change, many women have risen to new heights spiritually and been able to give great service to the world. For many life truly begins then. Always remember that you are a daughter of the Most High. Fearlessly let the old life of generation go and lay hold of the new life of freedom and peace. Keep your mind undisturbed, your heart clean and pure, your habits temperate and well ordered. You are being raised to a most precious expression of life.

Hold fast to God, the author and source of your life. He will bring you through this experience a new woman, triumphant, filled with the power of the Holy Spirit; radiant, alert with new incentive and understanding. Welcome your change, saying:

*Father, I thank Thee for the orderly adjustment of every function of my body. I thank Thee for the new life that I am entering. I willingly let go of the old and gladly lay hold of the new. Let Thy perfect*

## The Generative Organs

*will be done in me now.*

God's will for you is always peace, health, freedom, and joy. Every change that comes to you by His decree is good. It is fraught with limitless blessings of new life, light, and power.

Disorders peculiar to men and women can be relieved by Truth. In fact a higher, purer order of living, a more philosophical attitude toward life, a progressive study of Truth and application of its principles to the everyday life will restore order and health in these functions more quickly and permanently than any other treatment. Use a meditation such as this:

*I will to let God's pure life, order, and peace be made manifest in me. His spiritual substance purifies, redeems, and blesses my entire organism. I am lifted up, regenerated, and healed.*

# Busy Manufacturers

WITHIN YOU is the fountain of life. Your life is self-sustaining. Your supply and sustenance is momently provided. Nothing more clearly reveals this truth than the work your glands do for you.

We might liken the glands to a great chain of manufacturing centers and supply stations. They take the crude materials supplied to them by the blood and convert them into substances easily absorbed by your body, just as a saw mill takes great logs and converts them into lumber for the building of your home. Also they conserve certain materials until a demand for them arises and they supply certain natural remedies that keep the body in perfect order and repair.

Science has revealed that because of the perfect co-operation and co-ordination of its various parts the body is a unified whole. The more we study the body the more we appreciate this truth.

The more we study the world through the things that affect our daily life and well-being, the common things to which we are so accustomed that we accept them as a matter of course, the more we realize that the world, too, is a unified whole. All things work together in divine order and harmony.

## Busy Manufacturers

Silently, reverently we direct our thoughts within and there we discover at work within us the same principle of light, order, and life that directs the universe. We find that all organs, functions, cells, and glands work together to sustain us in perfect health and harmony. We know without doubt or question that our body is the temple of the living God; the world is the environment He has provided for our present habitation; and the universe is the expression of His Spirit. All is a unified whole.

Centers of life and light are active everywhere, absorbing elemental substance from sunshine, water, atmosphere, and soil, and converting it into other forms of substance for our blessing. Within our mind this same power and intelligence is at work converting the Christ word into living thought substance, giving it forth for the blessing of the people in thoughts, words, and deeds of loving-kindness.

Penetrating all things is a great system of supply, appropriation, and elimination that gives assurance of omnipresent substance to nourish and sustain all things, according to their needs.

Two seeds may lie side by side in the ground. One will draw from the earth the requisites for a towering tree. The other will produce new shoots of grass. Yet both take their substance from the same life source.

Likewise one gland in the body may supply digestants, another lubricants, another purifiers, another moisture, and so on, until every possible need of the body is met, but all draw their substance from the same blood or life stream.

There is no dearth of supply anywhere. The air you breathe is invisible, yet it provides elements essential to your life and to your world. Whether you can see them with the outer eye or not, infinite supply stations surround you in all directions. All your needs are fulfilled in Spirit.

Just as all things in the world work together for your good when you work with them in the spirit of divine order and harmony, so your glands work together to supply every cell in your body with the requisites of health. Thank God for them and bless them, saying:

*Glands of my body, wonder stations of service, purification, supply, and control, I now behold the perfect work of Spirit carried on through you. God has blessed you every one with His intelligence. I know you are working together for my good and I am working with you in the wisdom and harmony of Spirit. Everything I need is now supplied. Every gland is functioning perfectly because it is established in divine order and directed by divine intelligence. Every one is clean, harmonious, and healthy.*

God is your perfect life and substance.

# *Healing Light*

*PURE RAYS of divine light shine clearly in and through every cell in my body. The healing light of God penetrates and banishes all darkness, obscurity, and disease. My life, love, will, and desire are lifted up into the clear shining of God's light, and I am healed.*

The realization of light is essential to the healing of any false growth, especially if it is considered malignant or cancerous. It is surprising to know how many persons fear cancer, even though they have not the slightest symptom of it. Much of the fear and dread of this disease is due to the obscurity of its cause and the uncertainty of cure through medical means. Patients react to the uncertainty of the outcome and lose hope, thus shadowing their minds from the clear shining light of divine faith and love.

Radium and various electrical rays have been widely used. They symbolize the inner light that lights every man coming into the world and are infinitesimal in power compared with the healing light of God.

There is substance in the emanation of light that springs from the Holy Spirit of God within you. It does not burn and consume tissue but purifies and restores it to its primal perfection in the substance of being.

If you have any fear concerning cancer, any need to be healed of it or of hereditary beliefs about it, or a desire to help some other person regain health, turn on the light of God within! Give your good, your God indwelling, a chance to shine forth as wholeness.

The light of God in its full power and glory is the aggregate of every God quality shining in a steady ray of divine illumination. In this light nothing is obscure, nothing is incurable. In it are the issues of perfect life. In it wholeness is revealed.

Children and babies are considered immune to cancer. It is a disease that appears later in life after troubled, devitalizing thoughts of uncertainty or fear, unforgiveness or discouragement, discontent or rebellion have been built into the consciousness.

Thoughts of injustice and self-pity, frightened thoughts of disease or death appropriate the substance of the mind just as the cells of false growths appropriate the substance of the body. The one outpictures the other. They can and must be corrected, but that is no cause for great alarm. Alarm only aggravates the condition. It is a demand of the body for healing, a demand of the mind for renewal in Truth, a call from Spirit to return to God and receive from Him your complete restoration in mind, body, and soul.

*Healing Light*

When Jesus was transfigured before His apostles, they saw Him in the true body of light. Even His raiment was radiant with light. Turn your thoughts to the light of God. Do not dwell on the condition you wish to heal, do not discuss it with others, and do not delve into your mind in retrospective search for some error thought or memory.

Keep your mind fixed on the light of God. Let your thoughts be centered in the light of Truth. When you press the switch and flood your home with light, when you carry a torch with you in the darkness, when you look into the glow of your hearth fire, or see the sun shining across your room; whenever or wherever you behold light, remember that it comes to you as a bearer of healing tidings. It is a reminder, a symbol of the light of life that God has set up within your soul. Nothing can take it from you.

*Pure rays of divine light shine clearly in and through every cell in your body. The healing light of God penetrates and banishes all darkness, obscurity, error, and disease. Your life, love, will, and desire are lifted up into the clear shining of God's light, and you are healed.*

# He Bindeth Up Wounds

"I WILL RESTORE health unto thee, and I will heal thee of thy wounds."

The Spirit of divine love binds up all wounds with the healing grace of divine understanding.

Wounds of mind and heart are as grievous as are those of the flesh. When the mind is freed from irritating thoughts and occupied with thoughts of good will, when the heart that was torn by misunderstanding and grief is filled with love, comfort, and forgiveness, the wounds of the flesh that had been pronounced incurable are frequently healed.

A woman was suffering from a severe radium burn. It had eaten deep into the flesh above her heart. She longed to write to Silent Unity for help in prayer but was physically unable to do so. With her finger she traced the words on the coverlet of her bed, "Jesus Christ and Silent Unity please help me." Although her flesh was in anguish a great peace quieted her. Thoughts of fear that had gripped her mind gave way before the promise that came to her with such power that it seemed as though it had been spoken from within her own body: *"I will restore health unto thee, and I will heal thee of thy wounds."* In twelve hours ribs that had been

## He Bindeth Up Wounds

exposed were covered, in twenty-four hours flesh was building in, in forty-eight hours the woman was up and carrying on some strenuous physical work. When questioned about her miraculous recovery, she said quite simply, "God restored my health to me, and He healed me of my wound."

*"I will restore health unto thee, and I will heal thee of thy wounds."* You can accept this promise. You can be healed of any wound, no matter what its cause or nature. You can speak the word for others. You can pass on to them the healing, restorative, forgiving love of God.

Undoubtedly you understand something of first-aid treatment, so you know how carefully wounds should be cleansed. You know the importance of using clean, sterilized dressings, but have you ever realized that you can use Truth also for first aid? As you seek to be healed or to help others, relax in mind and in body and let the pure, cleansing, forgiving love of God permeate you. Treat the wound with thoughts of wholeness; seal it with faith that holds not the least atom of doubt or fear. It is as essential to keep fear, condemnation, despair, and worry out of your thoughts as it is to keep unsterilized dressings away from a wound. Lay hold of God's restorative life and substance. Let God be your first aid.

Great intelligence is revealed by the tissues of the body in the healing of a wound. Work with this intelligence. All the resources of Divine Mind are at your command. Speak authoritatively to your body. Bless it with quickening words of faith. Thank God for a perfect body free from blemish or scar. Thank Him for a perfect mind, for a heart filled with love and understanding.

The protective love of God surrounds you, upbuilding thoughts of Truth fill your mind, the healing Christ word of life is spoken through you. The promise is being fulfilled: *"I will restore health unto thee, I will heal thee of thy wounds."*

God, the mighty Healer, is not far from you. He is with you now. The blessing of His Holy Spirit is upon you. His love bridges every gap of misunderstanding. It closes and heals every wound.

"Let all flesh bless his holy name."

# The Seamless Robe

I LIKE TO think of the skin as the garment of righteousness and peace, the seamless robe of beauty, the reflector of the inner light of Spirit. I like to think of Jesus, Moses, and Stephen and the way in which their faces shone. The light of Truth shone forth in the radiance of their countenances, just as it shines today in the faces of those who love God and walk with Him.

The skin symbolizes divine protection. It is the protective covering of the deeper tissues of the body. It is quickly responsive to outer conditions and ever sensitive to the life within. Your reaction to the atmosphere of the world about you as well as to the radiation of light from the inner Christ realm has much to do with the condition of your skin.

Nearly every nerve center in the body may be affected by sensations arising in the skin. We are told that the surface of the skin is a mosaic of tiny sensory areas. Thus your skin warns you away from certain dangers. Also it has much to do with regulating the heat of your body, making it responsive to warmth and cold.

Pain is not desirable. However it is protective in its action, for it directs or even compels one who is in need of healing to be still and rest in order that the necessary healing work may be carried on within the body. It reminds him to heed again the inner voice of the divine counselor who directs, " 'Be still, and know that I am God.' Be still and know that I am your life, your peace. Be still, and know your perfect wholeness."

A need for healing is quickly brought to the attention of the physical man through several million pain points in the skin. Think of this marvelous protection provided for the life and health of the body. Several million reporters ever on the alert, working for the good of your body. Look at your skin and thank God for the living, intelligent garment that clothes you.

The beauty and grace of the indwelling Christ shines forth through you. Every nerve lying close to the surface of your body is carrying the message of your innermost thought out into your world.

There is a holy of holies within you. It is the secret place where God abides, where His image of perfection is kept before you, the pattern by which you bring forth His perfect likeness.

Have you ever watched a weaver working? Have you seen the tiny strands take shape in a lovely pattern? God in the midst of you is weaving His pattern of light, peace, and wholeness. He is clothing you round with infinite love and wisdom. The covering of your body temple is radiant with the light of His Holy Spirit.

*The Seamless Robe* 175

Indelibly stamped upon the skin covering your finger tips are tiny lines that always identify you. Indelibly stamped upon your heart are impressions eternally identifying you with God in the midst of you. Be still and let God make Himself known to you. Then as you go about your daily business of living let God be identified through you in the life you live. Your very flesh will reveal Him as life and substance. Your skin will glow with perfect health. Sebaceous glands will respond to your joy of living. They will keep your body perfectly anointed so that your skin may be soft, smooth, flexible, and beautiful as a child's. Every sweat gland of your body will function properly, and your body temperature will remain even and normal.

Your skin is in constant contact with the world. It is the immediate environment of your body. Whatever you give forth comes back to you again. Give forth blessings of understanding and good will and they will return to you every one. As you let go of resistant, cross, and irritable thoughts and radiate love and good will in their place, you will find a spirit of peace and satisfaction blessing your mind and healing the blemishes on your skin.

Do you recall the story of how the viper came out from a bundle of sticks and attached itself to Paul's hand? Those who were with Paul expected him to fall dead, but he remained unharmed. This shows that there is a divinity within man that makes him resistant to poisons of any kind.

Naturally, normally the healthy skin is a defense against many species of bacteria, which are impotent when they come in contact with such a skin.

Fear interferes with the proper functioning of your skin. Fear and dislike open the way for bee stings and annoyance from gnats and similar pests. Do not be careless about poison ivy or the like, but do not shrink from it in fear or expect to be harmed by it. There is a power in you greater than any power in the world. Train yourself to react fearlessly and calmly to the things of the world about you, and they will not harm you. Love harmonizes you with your earthly environment.

Quite frequently the question arises as to whether birthmarks, scars, brown spots, or freckles can be cleared away by Truth. Certainly they can. In Spirit you are unblemished, perfect. Physically your skin is being constantly renewed. You do not have to let your thoughts reproduce old conditions. You do not have to attach your faith to anything less than the perfect manifestation. You need not carry old scars, birthmarks, or discolorations with you any more than you need to carry old mistaken beliefs. "Ye shall know the truth, and the truth shall make you free." God, the Alpha and Omega, the beginning and the completion of all perfection, is working in you. He is redeeming you from every imperfection. Imperfections are outgrown when the trend of one's thoughts

## The Seamless Robe

and the mode of one's living is directed toward God and His perfection.

You have entered a new life in Christ. Old things have passed away. Misconceptions are being cleared from your mind. Imperfections are being corrected throughout your entire consciousness and your entire body. God is clothing you in the beauty, the grace, and the glory of righteousness and Truth.

As you daily bathe your body and keep it sweet and clean, bless your skin with thoughts such as these:

*God clothes me with His life and wholeness. I am infolded in His love and wisdom. The oil of joy and gladness makes beautiful the covering of my body. Peace, purity, love, and joy shine forth in every part of it. My skin takes on the substance of the Holy Spirit. Day by day it is renewed and made smooth, soft, clear, and perfect. Day by day I praise God for my seamless robe of radiant health and life.*

# Your Crown of Beauty

YOUR HAIR symbolizes life and strength. Bless it daily in Truth, and it will become a crown of beauty.

You are familiar with the story of Samson and how his strength left when his hair was cut. Undoubtedly you have known of those whose hair fell out when their strength was depleted because of illness, fever, or worry. In response to some great stress hair has been known to turn white overnight and in times of great alarm to stand on end. Hair is also responsive to thoughts of life, safety, and well-being.

Many times the question is asked "Has hair ever been restored through Truth?" It has been in many instances, both in color and quantity. I knew a woman past eighty, completely bald for more than two years, who grew new hair. Her hair came in as soft and perfect as a child's, and she said it was the exact color that it had been when she was a young woman. It grew rapidly and was luxuriant. She called it her "crown of life." As she brushed and cared for it she said it was as though new life flowed through her entire body.

If your scalp is tight and tense and your hair is thin and scraggly, remember that you do not do all

## Your Crown of Beauty

your thinking in your head. Use freely the knowledge you have gained. Know that intelligence is evenly distributed through your body. You do not have to cram your head with conscious anxieties, neither do you have to think for others. If you have children, teach them to think for themselves.

Do you know that you can make so simple a thing as brushing and combing your hair a life-renewing treatment? You can; and it will pay you well to do so not alone because of the increase of life, light, and beauty that will show forth in your hair, but because of the general good effect it will have in your mind, body, and affairs.

How would you like your hair to grow? Surely in beautiful abundance, luxuriant, glinting with light, free from dandruff, soft and manageable.

Try this method of blessing your hair and prove what it will do for you. With each stroke of comb or brush speak the word "life, life, life." You cannot do this and retain thoughts of weakness, weariness, age, baldness, or lack. Within a short time just the thought of brushing your hair will cause your scalp to tingle, and you will feel a glow of new life through your whole body.

Soon your heart will add its song of joy, freedom, love, and abundance to your thought of life. The Spirit of eternal life will vibrate through your word. Your hair, countenance, and body will respond with new beauty.

Think of the kind of hair you would like to have and retain. Do not try to force it to be exactly like another person's. Bless your hair with the Truth you know, and it will grow in an individual and beautiful manner most becoming to your physical type.

Amplify your word of life until you wield your hairbrush to a jolly roundelay of such words as vim, vigor, vitality; beautiful, bountiful, radiant, glorious; youthful, gleaming, silken, luxurious.

Think of your hair as God's protective mantle of life covering your head.

Even as every hair of your head is numbered, so does every hair bear witness to your rich inheritance of life and supply. Every time you comb your hair you will set into action an inner battery of life. It is frequently in the small commonplace and recurrent duties of our daily life that we come in touch with the vitality of the ever-renewing Spirit of life that abides in us.

Bless your body with the thought of divine order and balance in all its functions and activities, and you will not be troubled by superfluous hair. Grow day by day in recognition of Truth.

# Away with Epidemics!

GOOD HEALTH is not subject to variation. It is not here one minute and gone the next. Good health is the orderly and constant expression of God life. God Himself has established it in you.

*God is your health.* Are you willing to accept this Truth, to rely on it, to prove it? You are then immune from disease, secure from any form of epidemic, a torchbearer of the Jesus Christ gospel of life and wholeness.

"Thou shalt not be afraid . . .

Thou hast made the Most High thy habitation; There shall no evil befall thee."

*"God is my health."* You can begin this very moment to prove this Truth, to enjoy the assurance of abiding health. It will free your mind from every thought of fear concerning disease and protect you from it.

Disease loses its hold as man looks to God as the Spirit of wholeness and knows Him as health. Again and again in times of epidemics we hear or read of those who work in the midst of contagion unafraid, restoring order, harmony, and wholeness where chaos, fear, and disease reigned. They remain unharmed because their faith and thought is centered in God's life and wholeness.

Just as strikes are frequently the result of the mass thought of injustice and insufficiency, so epidemics are the result of the mass thought of disease. Fear thoughts working in the minds of the people who have been educated from earliest childhood to believe in disease create fearsome conditions.

Charles Fillmore says, "Disease germs created and named by the intellect of man bear within themselves sufficient intelligence to answer to the name given to them, and to come when they are called."

When a community, a household, or an individual learns to know God as health and wholeness, health and wholeness are called forth and made manifest to others. Health is stronger than disease and even more readily communicated. In the days of the disciples sick folk were carried and placed where the shadow of Peter might fall over them. What a consciousness of health and wholeness Peter must have gained from the Master!

*"God is my health."* Be sure of this within your own mind and heart. Then make a daily practice of blessing all who come into your environment in thought or in person with the word *God is your health*. Quietly, confidently, peacefully know for yourself and others, and especially for little children: *God is your health*.

You can truly prove God as your health. Many others have done it. You can do it. Truth makes you

## Away with Epidemics! 183

strong, fearless, and healthy. It makes your mind, heart, service, and environment wholesome and orderly.

Let us work together to free the race from epidemics, to lift from babies and children the yoke of diseases commonly associated with childhood. Let us turn thumbs down on mumps, measles, whooping cough, and the like, and know for our little ones, and teach them to know, that God is their health. Let us call forth, in the name of the Son, the perfect life and wholeness of our Father-God.

Away with contagion and its demands. Away with ignorance, bondage, and fear! Let the kingdom of Jesus Christ be ushered in and the reign of wholeness be established. Let Truth be made known to all mankind.

*God is our health.*

# Wholeness for You

WHOLENESS is God's will for you. Let wholeness be your will for your body. Do not let anything come between you and your spiritual determination to be perfectly well and strong.

Should you have any doubt that restoration, health, and strength are God's will for you or anyone else, sit down quietly with your Bible and with an unbiased mind read the four Gospels. Trace the divine purpose back of the ministry of Jesus. You will find every lesson, every parable, every miracle, every word directing you toward peace of mind and wholeness.

The ministry of Jesus was founded on healing; healing of mind, body, and soul—as well as healing of nations. Who will say that in His mighty service of healing Jesus was working against God's will? Not one. God's will is wholeness.

Holiness is the outworking of God's will in the mind and soul; wholeness is the acceptance of His will in the body; abundance of all good is the outworking of His will in one's affairs and environment.

The personal ministry of Jesus was short. It lasted but a few years after His baptism. Yet His words and deeds so quickened the minds of His fol-

*Wholeness for You* 185

lowers that those whom He taught passed His teachings on to others; those whom He healed kept His healing ministry alive; those who felt the power of His love talked and sang and wrote of it until now the whole world knows about Christ.

Every person is as a cell in the universal Christ body, so close are we to Him. The work of Christ will not be completed until every cell, every soul and body, is radiant with love that portrays the fullness and glory of divine life. His work will continue until everybody is perfect and whole. Let your life shine with the fullness of His love for you, His joy in you. Do not delay His perfect healing work by a single retarding doubt.

Christ abides in you to enable you to carry out God's will of wholeness; to fill you with the consciousness of life, light, and joy so that every cell in your body will respond to His word and relay to you again His living message. Thus shall His word become flesh and perfect you in the beauty of holiness.

Your heart is the channel of His love; your mind the focal point of His teachings; the cells of your body the living messengers of His gospel of wholeness.

Have you seen, do you now know the object of these healing blessings? They have been written for you not alone for the purpose of helping you to become established in an abiding consciousness of good health, but also to quicken your appreciation of your body as the living temple of God until every cell becomes to you a symbol of spiritual wholeness and holiness.

As you have blessed and appreciated them, your eyes have come to mean something more than mere organs of sight. They remind you of God's vision, the perfection He beholds. Your ears are no longer just the medium of hearing, they are receivers of His good tidings of joy. Your heart is something more than a blood-pumping station; it has become to you the abode of divine love, and every pulse beat reminds you of God's love for you. Your voice reminds you of the power of the spoken word; your hands outpicture the willing service of Jesus Christ; every muscle teaches you obedience; and so on through your entire body. Do you not see how your body is an open book of life constantly teaching you lessons of wisdom, order, harmony, continually blessing you with joy and freedom?

It is joyous; it is free; it is wonderful to live in a body glowing with the light and love of your blessing, a body that is truly becoming the manifestation of God life and wholeness, in which every organ, function, and cell sends back to you in increased measure the blessing that through your faith in your indwelling Lord you have given to it.

Some cells in your body may be more quickly esponsive to the word of life than others, just as

## Wholeness for You

some people are, but that need not deter you from trying by thought, word, and deed to carry out God's will in every part of your body. Above the din of doubt, fear, ridicule, the Christ indwelling is calling to you, "Be thou made whole."

*God's will for you is wholeness. Now may His perfect will be done in you, and your perfect body shine forth in the joy and glory of divine wholeness. God's song of life, His song of love and power, is quickened in your soul. It is ever healing and harmonizing you. It is blessing you now and forever, and every part of your being pays tribute to God in the beauty of holiness.*

## CHRIST'S BENEDICTION

*"Peace I leave with you; my peace I give unto you: not as the world giveth, give I unto you. Let not your heart be troubled, neither let it be fearful." "Lo, I am with you always."*

Printed U.S.A.
23-F-5339-3M-2-82

Thirteenth Printing